11-23-90

To Mike,

Thank you for the
wonderful letter that
saved days life —
I appreciate your trust
and faith me
Hope you enjoy my
Book —

HEART TO HEART

Also by Ed Storti

Crisis Intervention

HEART TO HEART

THE HONORABLE APPROACH TO MOTIVATIONAL INTERVENTION

Ed Storti

WITH SANDY VON WOLFFRADT

A Hearthstone Book

Carlton Press Corp.   New York, N.Y.

Dedicated to Jo Ann, Karianne and Kristopher

C O N T E N T S

Acknowledgments

When you write a book, it crosses your mind how many colleagues and friends you have. There are so many people who were so dedicated and supportive of myself and others that I must acknowledge a few of them.

To my wife, Jo Ann, for her love and support, her unconditional giving to me. If it were not for Jo Ann, I'd not be where I am today . . . . Thank you, Jo.

Thank you to Mary Margaret Lorrenzi. Words cannot describe her dedication and devotion to families and her continuous support day in and day out, in being the air traffic controller, in directing and shifting my cases . . . rack 'em, pack 'em and stack 'em, Mary Margaret.

To Sandy von Wolffradt for being that special word-smith that put all my words together and made sense of them. I thank you.

To Dottie Braxton for helping in the editing of my manuscript and her never-ending support at Las Encinas Hospital. Also, to Terry Gannon for her enthusiasm and belief in me and my work. To Roland Metivier for his trust and faith and wonderful support. To Dr. Tom McCain for being one of my heroes, and Bruce Kreiger for his devotion and kindness in helping I.L.W.U. members. To Jackie Cummings for her dedication and compassion in helping so many suffering families; Dr. Leland Whitson and Dr. Bruce Walker for their contribution in the field of addictive disease; Fred DiBernardo for his legal advice and counsel throughout the years.

To Laura Potier for continuous belief in me over the years; Linda Jirava for her professionalism; Cheryl Brown for her dedication and support; Malcom Butler for his trust and faith in me; Richard Rogg for his love and passion in treating the addict; Dr. Joanne Barge for introducing me to U.C.L.A. and continuous support in my career. To Conrad Watson for being a man that walks the walk . . . he's an inspiration; Julie Kelly for her unconditional love and support and Steve Jackson for his friendship and continuous giving. To Saints Jude and Joseph . . . thanks! To Gerry McDonald . . . let's keep on trudgin'!

To the many dedicated and kind colleagues that have been there for me over the years . . . . THIS ONE IS FOR YOU!

The following Statement of Purpose was sent to me and all participants of a particular intervention in 1983. I share it here because its poignant sentiment is one I've found applicable to all interventions.

There's an old movie about an over-the-hill airplane pilot (John Wayne) who crashes in the wilds of Alaska. When his comrades of WWII hear about it, they pass the word, "Dooley's down." It is high drama and very touching when each comrade responds to the call.

Our "Dooley" is down. Those who cannot be physically present at the intervention will be present in spirit, heart and soul. That's what's important.

This is for "Dooley." May the warm spirit of brotherhood that has been omnipresent in this effort prevail through the intervention and for the critical days ahead. You know, "Ole Dooley" is just flat worth giving it our best shot.

P.S. You guessed it; John Wayne was rescued.

Introduction

I can think of nothing more painful than the tragic plight of a fellow human being, and nothing more gratifying than being a part of the solution for that person. In a nutshell, I guess that's why I became an intervention specialist.

I started "intervening" over nineteen years ago when I was working with probationary youth in the San Pedro area of Los Angeles. That was before I had any labels for my methods, or any official procedures. My first intervention case in the field of addictive disease presented itself when a weary father approached me in Palos Verdes, California, and asked for help with his twenty-three-year-old alcoholic daughter. The man was clearly at the end of his rope; it showed in his tired posture, his cracked voice, and, most of all, in his sad, evasive eyes. He had come to me as a last resort, having exhausted every other method he'd heard about to help get his daughter on the road to recovery. He wasn't angry or disgusted with her—quite the contrary; he was afraid to lose her, afraid it wouldn't be long before she died of this chronic, progressive disease of alcoholism.

Not having intervened in a situation like this before, I consulted my peers in the therapy field.

"Don't do it," they said. "There's no use until the girl bottoms out and comes (crawling) to you." My colleagues also warned me against going to the person's home, but when I spoke to the father again, I was too moved by his despair to say I couldn't help. I offered to speak with his daughter, believing that she was incapable of deciding on her own that she needed help.

"You'd do that for me?" her father asked incredulously. He had gotten used to being told his daughter would have to make the first move.

"I'll give it a shot," I said. "I can't guarantee any results, but I'll come and talk to her."

The next night, while I trembled on her doorstep and tried to swallow with a throat as dry as the Sahara, I wondered what I was doing there. I didn't have a clue as to what I planned on saying. Who was I to buck a system (of intervention and counseling) I hadn't even tried yet? Was I crazy or arrogant or what? Then I looked at her father's face and I melted inside. That's why I had come.

The door opened and I introduced myself and asked if I could speak to her for a few minutes. She let me in and I talked to her as if we'd been friends for years—no accusations, no threats. I just spoke from my heart and told her how much she was loved by her father, and presented hope to her in the form of going to a treatment center. She agreed, and I was stunned and grateful. So this is what it's all about, I thought. One person helping another. No titles, no labels, no shoulds or shouldn'ts. Just plain, sincere talk.

In 1988, I became a published author with *Crisis Intervention*, a book about my intervention experiences over the past fifteen years. But even as I read the galley proofs for the manuscript, I felt a gnawing in my gut that something was missing. Even though the interventions had been successful and the true-life people stories were inspiring, I didn't have the process and dynamics of the intervention clearly spelled out. I wasn't as crystallized in my thinking or in the procedure as I am today. I guess that's growth and that's where this book comes in.

Heart to Heart: The Honorable Approach to Motivational Intervention is primarily a "cookbook" for those wanting to get a thorough understanding of the intervention process. The book describes intervention as a tool to help the lay public, paraprofessionals, and established professionals. It is a "quick read" intended to acquaint the reader to my method of intervention—sort of a bird's-eye view of the Storti intervention process.

I say "Heart to Heart" because that's the bottom line. That's what makes my method work for me. Only you can describe how it might work for you. There are many methods of intervening; I call my method the "honorable approach" because it is designed as a gift for the guest of honor who happens to be addicted to one kind of substance or another.

I was never taught or instructed in the how-to of a chemical dependency intervention. Instead, my method has developed from the questions, responses and needs of those I've attended to. What is an intervention, how does it work, what are the risks, do I have to be prepared to get a divorce? These questions and many similar ones were put to me over and over again by the public, including both patients and family audiences. Most of the answers are given in the initial assessment to determine if an intervention is the best course of action to take. This book has been prepared as a preliminary guide. That way, once a person investigates the possibility of an intervention with a specialist, the overall procedures, goals, and risks will already be identified.

For the sake of simplicity, and meaning no bias, I have used the pronoun "he" throughout the book. The reality is that men and women are equally vulnerable to and caught in a progressive, addictive lifestyle.

One of the strengths of an intervention is the gathering of loved ones to surround the dependent person. Each loved one tries to bring home to the chemically dependent the reality of his or her addiction and, hopefully, spur him or her to take action immediately by accepting treatment. As humans, we are predisposed to listen selectively—that's one reason interventions are so successful. Each participant who speaks to the dependent may say the same thing ("We love you and want you to get help"), but each loved one does so in his own words and that's the key to getting through to the addicted person. It's somewhat like the good advice you got about life insurance. "Buy it now while you're still young—it will grow bigger and faster, and the premiums will be cheaper." But if you're like most people, you put it off until you're approaching forty years of age. Then, you start to see the value in it and the wisdom of buying it early and by the time you're sixty the truth hits you right between the eyes. It finally sinks in—you just needed to hear it at different times, in different ways. That's the way it is with the intervention process; you may find some of the information repeated at various points and in different ways throughout the book, but I feel it's necessary to get the message across and to give you a sense of the whole picture. So please bear with me and trust the process.

As my good friend Gerry Mc once said, "You tell 'em what you're going to tell 'em, then you tell 'em, and then you tell 'em what you just told 'em."

I invite you to read this in an effort to get an overview of the intervention procedure, the risks and benefits of an intervention, and to consider how an intervention might be the most powerful gift you could give to someone you love.

HEART TO HEART

"You Asked for It!"

Between eighteen and twenty-two million people suffer with addictive diseases. That's amazing when you consider an addictive disease is the most treatable kind. (In fact, if you were going to buy a disease, chemical dependency is not a bad one to choose—because it is treatable.) But the sad truth, as most recent studies have shown us, is that less than 15 percent (or approximately three million) will actually get help. The gap between treatment and the patient is a wide and tragic reality in our world. Most people cling to their addiction like a baby to its mother, and it's only when the secondary manifestations (such as loss of job, divorce, accident, etc.) smack the person in the face that the disease might be addressed. Even then, the addicted person, the family, and often the professional as well focus only on the "immediate" problem, rather than looking at what's actually causing the problem. In other words, it's one thing to treat the fever and quite another to treat the cause. Addictive disease is terminal, but most people don't really believe that until they're actually in the shadow of death.

There are several myths about chemical dependency intervention that often keeps it ignored as an option. One myth is that the addicted person must bottom out before he can accept treatment for the disease. This is like saying, "We'll hold off on the brain tumor surgery a while longer, because the patient hasn't deteriorated enough yet." In every other major disease, from cancer and AIDS to leukemia, early detection and treatment is stressed both to prevent the progression of the disease and to possibly gain remission. Addictive diseases, however, are still not generally accepted by the public as physical illnesses and, thus, intervention is not accepted as the penicillin or antibiotic medicine that it could be. Professionals still turn families away with advice to "get help for yourself," and just "wait" for the patient to want to get help. Let them fall and you take care of yourself.

In one case in which a young man had given up on himself, surrendered to his addiction, and was only waiting for Death to finally free him, his friend participated in an intervention for him. "Look, Larry," the friend said gently, "if you don't care enough for yourself, think about all of us who love you. My little girls adore you—you're their godfather and I hate to think how your disease will affect them." The picture of those two little girls smiling up at him brought the young man around and he got help.

Not long after, he was asked his opinion about the idea of having to bottom out before getting help. He said quite simply, "If they had waited for me to want to help myself, and go get help on my own, I'd be dead today." The addiction precludes rational thought—he was incapable of making any such decision.

In another case, a family had lost a twenty-year-old boy to an overdose of drugs, and the family was devastated for not having tried an intervention before it was too late. They said, "We could have accepted 'yes or no' but now we'll never know."

Another common myth is that interventions must be heavy-handed, an emotional SWAT team that's prepared to fire an "or else" at the patient. "You go to treatment or else never step foot in my house again." "Get help or else you're fired." "Accept this treatment or I'm walking out and getting a divorce." Some intervention styles employ this sort of leverage with the patient and it can be effective at times, but it's not a mandatory part of an intervention and it's not a part of the Storti method. An intervention is a frightening and awkward ordeal in itself—to threaten overt actions asks too much, too fast, of the family, and it winds up only instilling fear in everyone.

The idea that paying for treatment (spending money on it) out of your own pocket is tied directly to the recovery results is another falsehood. Families often think the patient will be more inclined to go and stay with the treatment center if he or she pays for it. The theory is that money is the motivator and that if someone else pays for the treatment, it's not as important to you as it would be if you were paying for it yourself. This is simply not true. In fact, the reverse is often the case. When a group has united to offer this (paid) gift to the addicted one, he or she is uplifted by the spirit of their caring and newly inspired to follow through with treatment. Starting treatment is like the horse being led to water. Whether the patient drinks the water or not is his decision. No one can force you to love yourself and accept all that treatment can give you. Yet once the patient has been treated, there is a healthy imprint that has been recorded and the patient normally will never be the same.

THE DISEASE

There are innumerable sources of excellent information about addictive disease and compulsive/obsessive behavior; this book won't duplicate those efforts to inform and educate. But in speaking about disease in general, there are certain common elements that are important to acknowledge.

1. **Progressive**—the disease gets worse and worse over time whether it is physiological or psychological in the case of compulsive/obsessive behavior. There is no cure; the goal is to gain remission and live a healthy life.

2. **Chronic**—the disease can remain in the background for years, ever overshadowing the person's life, before the body starts showing decay or the disease becomes acute

3. **Predictable, definable**—the direction and consequences of the disease are standard. We know what will happen; it's just a matter of time. There is another common myth among the public called "sincere delusion"; people believe that the addict sees the same reality that they do. In truth, the dependent is sincere in his belief that "things will get better" but doesn't really see (or share) the reality of the situation—things don't

look as bad as they really are. This delusion also works for the family in that it allows the family to think he or she is different from the rest and can therefore "take care of it their way."

4. **Pain**—Addicted persons have a very high tolerance for pain and self-abuse. If they saw somebody treating someone else the way they treated themselves, they would call it cruel and demand it be stopped. But for themselves, they think it's "not so bad, it's tolerable." This is what I call the frying pan theory—the addict has a certain excitement when sitting in the frying pan. They need to feel the heat. You warn the chemical dependent not to touch the burner on the stovetop because it's too hot—the addict will want to touch it immediately to see what it feels like to get burned. (There is addiction to pain.)

In summary, the disease of addiction is like a broken filter. Just as the pancreas in the diabetic cannot produce insulin, there is a filter in the neuro-transmitters of the brain that cannot accept x amount of alcohol (or any other drug) and still function properly for some people. And just as diabetes isn't an illness everyone has, the intolerance for alcohol and/or drugs or other substances doesn't happen for everyone. Each individual has his own tolerance level for the drug of choice and normally, it builds up over time and through age, with the person typically digressing in his/her tolerance of the substance. Yet, when that tolerance level peaks, and the imaginary line is crossed, the person will experience varying degrees of blackouts, fuzzy memory, repetitive conversation, physical deterioration, family deterioration, and social isolation. From this point on, the patient has virtually an allergy to all mood-altering substances. Dependency is a well-guarded secret of the addict and most addicts will keep their guard up (especially while in public) until the disease becomes too blatant for others to ignore.

There are certain character traits everyone has that are amplified when a person is addicted to a substance or abusive activity. The traits take enormous proportion in the mind of the person, signaling the brain to send down a kindly portion of the chosen drug to sedate the feelings beginning to surface. Pride, a tenacious but delicate thing, is one such trait that can get in the way of recovery. Being overly sensitive, holding on to resentment, taking life very seriously; a powerful intensity (or inflexible logic) often makes the addict see points A, B, C, and E, but he can't find point D. He will be obsessed with finding D with no consideration for doing what he wants without D.

Shyness, fear of the future, and rigidity of values are all tough issues that loom like monsters in the dark in the mind of an addicted person. And while the patient may be good-hearted, generous and kind, he is also often prone to taking those traits to the opposite extreme, becoming grandiose and manipulative. The desire for control, false ego, defiance and emotional adolescence come to the forefront of the person's thinking, which leads him to a psychological dependency, which permits him to use the drug of choice (for comfort and pain relief), which feeds back into the physiological dependency. The particular traits, including spiritual decay, loneliness, guilt, lack of honesty, people-pleasing, low self-esteem, and no self-love, need to be trimmed or tempered so that the person isn't tempted to enjoy the psychological dependency. Most relapses happen from erroneous or harmful thinking. Alcoholism is a combination of alcohol (the chemical substance) and "i-s-m" (the "I Sabotage Myself" mentality of the patient). The negative thinking leads the mighty psychological voice to say, "Here, take this or do that, and you'll feel better." Treating the whole disease of addiction is to treat the physical and psychological aspects, including the mind set of the person (coming to terms with the skeletons in the closet—we can be as sick as our deepest secrets).

FAMILY FRUSTRATION

As is true with the subject of disease, there are many, many good references for the study of family dynamics. In the context of understanding interventions (particularly, my motivational method), suffice it to say the family is extremely powerful. That's what makes the intervention inspirational—the public declaration of a family's love for one of its members. The deep intensity of caring individuals united to support one member is the main ingredient of the intervention presentation.

Despite the strength of the family, however, it is often the family members who have "bottomed out" rather than the addicted person. They can't live with the disease and what it does to their loved one (or themselves) any longer. They have been victimized by the disease through co-dependency (fixing, mending, enabling), financial deterioration, physical or verbal assault, or just being tired of being tired of everything for long enough. Values and dreams fade away as a loved one gets progressively worse. They are desperate for relief. They can't fight anymore.

It's up to the intervention specialist to consider the family's stability and health in the assessment and preparation for an intervention. Is the key person who is suggesting the intervention too fragile for the process? How unified is the nucleus of the group? How determined are they to lay the cards out on the table—honestly, sincerely, genuinely, and in a motivational manner? So often, they are afraid of what may happen if they don't take action. They want to give it "one last shot," if only for family and friends to know that they were unified under one roof, one moment, one day, with a solution for the patient and family.

NON-TRADITIONAL METHOD

There are several different types of intervention and virtually all models have certain advantages. The Storti method of intervention is only one method—it works for me and it may work for you. The primary purpose of this book is to help you see the basic components of an intervention so the Storti method can be considered as a solution, along with any other possibilities. This book is not saying this is the only way or the best way; the best way is the one you feel most comfortable with for your circumstance.

The Storti method differs from other models in several significant ways. First of all, it is an accelerated method (going from preparation to intervention in twelve to sixteen hours). This is, in large part, an answer to the "gotta have it now" attitude of our society. People don't have time to study the process and debate its variances; they need help now and they don't have a lot of time after they get together to plan and do the presentation. Another reason the quick schedule works best is that most participants' energy can be condensed in short periods of time, which provides a powerful dose of positive vitality and excitement to the intervention.

The Storti method takes into account whether the addicted person is a wealthy entrepreneur; an indigent, widowed housewife; a cattle rancher; a teenager; a construction worker; an attorney, or whatever. There are certain ways to motivate certain personalities. For the chemistry (and every other aspect of the intervention) to work advantageously, you have to have the right "mix" of people. The intervention specialist helps determine this "people combination," based on the unity, momentum, attitude and personality of the group, and modifies his/her own role accordingly. That is part of personalizing the intervention to the individual situation, another difference from traditional intervention methods.

The intervention specialist himself is a primary participant of the intervention, as he choreographs the presentation. He's the director as well as a role model for participants. The pace and rhythm, the timing of the intervention, are determined by the intervention specialist with careful consideration of the particular circumstance. In other methods, the specialist may totally dominate the presentation, or he may simply set the stage and fade into the background while family and other participants go their own way. The point is, different methods or different specialists generally have one style that is standard for their presentations. My method is to fluctuate according to the particular circumstances of the individual group and patient.

Another major difference between traditional intervention methods and the Storti method is that my method is done primarily in the home (or on the yacht or in the office) of the addicted individual. While this is a very unpopular way to go with other professionals, I believe it is actually the most natural. Going to the patient in his own environment eliminates schemes to get the person to go somewhere, avoiding deceit, and finds the individual much more relaxed and willing to listen in the comfort of his own surroundings.

One difference that was mentioned briefly earlier in the chapter is that the Storti method is motivational and inspiring. Serious confrontation, threats and demands, are replaced by warm, loving words spoken by people who truly care about the person. The Storti model lives up to its name in part because the group assembles and goes to meet the patient, putting him/her into the guest of honor role. A positive, upbeat energy generates the whole presentation, making the intervention a true gift in honor of the individual and one in which all the participants are glad and proud to have given.

The presentation is an unconditional one, staying in the solution phase of the intervention. Leverage or threatened punishment does not exist. Speaking from the heart is the way to plant the seed (that there is hope, there is a solution) in the mind of the addicted person. Even if the person doesn't accept the solution on the spot, the seed will have been planted and nothing will ever be the same. Silence surrounds addiction. The intervention fractures that silence—forever.

The participants are encouraged to speak from their

own hearts to the individual's heart, thus the heart-to-heart approach. (Why appeal to the mind when it's going in reverse?) Addressing the mind of the individual only opens the door for accusations, argument, injured pride and a host of other negative exchanges. Go for the heart. "We love you—we want to help. We honor you with this gift and we want to be honored by you accepting it today!" This is what the Storti intervention says.

Perhaps because the presentation is so carefully tailored to the individual, one of the other major differences between the Storti method and traditional models of intervention is the group bonding that occurs. The specialist must be sensitive to the needs of the group as well as of the patient. The presentation will ultimately bind any group to a certain extent, but it's the deeply moving intensity of caring about someone that casts a spell of sorts over the intervention and unites all the people involved as if they'd just witnessed a miracle together. And in essence, maybe they have.

These differences and others are what has developed into the Storti method of intervention. From that first nervous visit to the young lady whose father asked for my help to the present time, almost twenty years later, I created a business based on motivational intervention. I honestly believe that, once in treatment, an addicted person has 100 percent chance of remission. The treatment centers don't fail—patients who cannot accept that their addiction is a terminal disease, patients who opt to merely trade one addiction for another—those are the ones who write their own prescriptions for failure. The difference, then, between cancer and alcoholism is psychological and physical; it's the control of the remission. Once the physical addiction has been treated, the individual can choose to keep the disease in remission in his/her body. If only cancer patients (or people with muscular dystrophy, leukemia, or AIDS) had such an option!

A recent three-year study we did on 397 cases supports the overall success of intervention and treatment: 94 percent of the people intervened upon went to treatment immediately. Of the remaining ones (6 percent), who didn't go in for treatment, 80 percent of them did go sometime later, usually within twenty-four hours to three weeks later. We did a separate follow-up study with almost fifty-five families contacted between one and a half months to one and a half years after the intervention to check the status of the patient's recovery and discovered an 80 percent abstention rate. Nine people had relapsed at one point, but all of them were subsequently back on track and were abstaining at the time of the survey. It's evidence like this that makes the fact that there is such a wide gap between the chemically dependent and treatment so tragic. This book was written to help close that gap through the intervention technique!

VIGNETTE—THIS IS YOUR LIFE!

It was cold and gray, the San Francisco Bay area under its common winter fog, when I got off the plane to meet Christine. I recognized her at once despite the fact that we had never met in person. She stood tall and tense, dressed as casually as doctors' wives dare to in public, her shoulder-length frosted hair a pale gold and held in place with a tidy style and simple, but expensive clasp. I could tell last week by her voice on the phone that she was the quiet, eloquent type who tried to maintain the proper image at all costs. In this case, the cost was laughter, as Christine's adult daughter, Terry, had pointed out. There hadn't been any laughter in the house for years and now, her father's drinking was causing increasingly more bizarre behavior, blackouts and repetitive talk.

Christine had called to engage my help dealing with her fifty-two-year-old husband/surgeon who was addicted to alcohol and valium. She was alarmed by his periods of forgetfulness, afraid of his aggressive freeway driving and severe mood swings. She was afraid for herself and the family, and also for his patients. Sometimes he wouldn't even remember performing surgery and would call one of the other doctors to confirm his patient's prognosis and status. Then, there was the anniversary dinner for a close friend of theirs. When it came time for him to toast the couple, he stumbled up to the podium and told a vulgar, totally inappropriate joke in slurred, clumsy speech. Christine had confessed to me that she ran into the restroom and sat on the floor crying over what this addiction had done to the man she loved and to herself. Suddenly, she became aware she had been beaten in trying to protect John. It was out of control.

A week or so later, John took a walk out in the front yard totally nude! The neighbors were ready to call the police, fearing something awful in the house had driven him out—dressed or not. In truth, the doctor had thought he was wearing underwear; it was his normal habit to walk around the house in his underwear. That incident was the one that prompted Christine to call me.

We held a conference call with both adult children, Terry and John Junior. It was clear they still loved their father. John Junior wanted to do whatever he could to help, but Terry had grown much less tolerant of her father's drinking than her brother. Both would participate in the intervention.

The day had come—"already" to Christine but "finally" to Terry. I walked up from the airport gate to Christine and we drove over to the hotel for the preparation. The family tried unsuccessfully to get John's working partner physician to join us in the preparation. Although he noticed a decrease in the number of patients John was seeing, he hadn't seen any drug or alcohol abuse on the job. Knowing the importance of having a peer in the same field as the patient involved in the intervention, I was able to find another doctor who had been treated years ago who was willing to participate. Christine, John Junior, Terry, the other doctor, John's parents (both in their eighties) and Kumi, an old college buddy of John's, all assembled with me at the hotel to prepare for the intervention. I was also given five letters of encouragement to read from and one videotape from part of the family in Michigan who wanted to show their support.

Everyone saw the intervention as a last-chance attempt to help; they were willing because of the strong core of love and respect they each held for John. Kumi mentioned that John had had the same problem way back when they were taking science classes together in college. This was news to Christine.

We met in the hotel parking lot the next morning

and drove in a convoy to the doctor's house, looking somewhat like a drug enforcement raid as we wound around the mile-long driveway. We parked quietly and approached the house together and I rang the door bell. The door opened.

"Oh no," John said, "you're not going to do one of those intervention things, are you?" Casual words, but the hair on his arms and the back of his neck had risen noticeably.

I introduced myself and said we just wanted to talk to him for a few minutes. "Every one of these people came here today to bring you this honorable gift. All who are present here have stated that over the years you have given them significant and cherished support, and today, they want to give to you, by their time and energy, their honesty and a solution. So this is your day, and we honor you today by being here." He started to soften a little and I went on to bring in the other participants and some of the sentiment in the letters, but it was Terry's words that caught his attention.

"Dad, I love you so much," she said softly. "This is your life; it's your life. You brought me into this world and today I want to give life back to you in some small way. Today is a rebirth for you and I'm proud to be part of this solution."

It was a moment of joy and sorrow for John at once. I could tell he was ready to agree, except for—. There was a well of "yeah, buts" gathering in his head; the overwhelming one was his concern for his practice. How could he leave his patients and jeopardize his practice?

That's when the other doctor spoke up. "Your next patient may be your biggest malpractice lawsuit," he warned John. "I wish someone had done this for me. I lost my family and my practice before I got help."

Then John's father, Josip, spoke for himself and his wife. "You know, son, we love you and have always been proud of you. This intervention gives us a relief to know we helped present a solution before it was too late. We want you to know the joy of grandchildren like we have through you."

That did it. Out came the Kleenex and John allowed himself to be escorted to a private treatment center in the desert by his son, John Junior, and his friend Kumi. He took his daughter's words to heart as he boarded the plane thinking it was the first time in a long time that he was glad "this was his life."

Speaking from the Heart

A motivational intervention is a proud and won-derful experience to honor and inspire, as op-posed to forcing the recipient to accept the solution (treatment) as a gift. For the group, the goal is to be able to present the intervention with dignity and know that they have all given their time and energy, with commitment, under one roof and also to release the problem emotionally, so they, too, can get on with their lives. In essence, the process has a springboard effect in that it catapults the addict to another level, so he can begin to live life rather than merely endure it.

Basically, the group represents a foundation of en-ergy, rounding up the fragments that each individual brings and melding them together in one place for one moment. The power is in the unity, and once again, the whole is greater than the sum of the parts it's made of. In essence, we're saying, "For all the enabling and co-dependency spent over the years up to this point and what will be spent in the future, for the addict's sake (and ours), let's do it all together, now." We'll unstick the family as well as the chemically dependent not unlike the treatment as it is applied in a medical emergency. The physician in a triage minimizes the immediate bleeding or pain and then prepares the patient for full treatment. The family can then be reassured (a little) knowing that treatment is in process and their loved one's condition will be stabilized.

It is indeed an honor in which we met and intervened on a man in a hotel suite. He sat and he listened patiently and eventually he agreed. "I know you're right," he said, "but I need twenty-four hours to think about it." This is a fairly common reaction and the addicts who are intervened upon and refuse to accept treatment wind up going for treatment on their own later. So I started to wrap things up and I asked the man's wife if she would like to add anything. She hadn't wanted to speak until then and I'll never forget what she said that night. It is true for so many people.

"I've been sitting here listening to all this love and compassion given to you, the obvious deep respect each of them has for you, and all the wonderful thoughts and feelings they've expressed," she said. "Every single one of them took time out of their own schedules, time away from their own families to coordinate this and be here tonight—the least you can do is give them back twenty-four hours of your time. I just can't help wondering for myself, who in my life would care this much? I really can't say." The man finally recognized the place of honor he was in and went immediately into treatment.

In a similar speech, Dick Gregory once said to Richard Pryor at a Hollywood event given in Pryor's honor: "Richard, this is a very important group of people here. There are lots of other places every one of them could be. But they've chosen to be here for you tonight." He went on to say, "We love you and care for you and you mean everything to us. And when you come right down to it, one of the most wonderful gifts one person can give to another is to take time out of their lives to be with you."

It's true, and that's what my method of intervention is all about—giving time, love, compassion and a solution to a loved one.

SAME PROCEDURE/DIFFERENT DISEASES

Motivational intervention has been used successfully for many, many different types of addictive behavior—alcohol, drugs and food are the three most often addressed. Compulsive gambling or excessive spending (money), dysfunctional relationship addiction, sex addiction (anywhere from spending hours on "porn numbers" to cross-dressing to pornography books), smoking (nicotine), steroid use, moving an elderly loved one into a nursing home, and obsessive television viewing have all been troubles of people I have intervened on. Then there are the people with other medical illnesses, such as heart disease, diabetes and cancer, who have given up on themselves and surrendered to the disease.

The procedure is always the same; only the emphasis and issue-specific phrases and concerns are changed. We'll go into the actual procedure a little later, but I also want to mention that it's very common for the addict to be addicted to more than one substance or activity at once.

SPECIALIZED PROCEDURE

The intervention is designed to present a solution to one individual at a time; however, sometimes someone else in the group may also decide to go into treatment. I once received a call when I was a guest on a radio talk show, from a young man who said he had participated in one of my interventions for a friend of his last year, and had recently gone through treatment for himself because of the experience.

In another case, we intervened on a man who refused to accept the treatment. "I don't care what you say, I'm not going!" Then his wife popped up and said, "Well, I am." The husband then followed her in an outpatient program. Another time, a college student was being intervened on for drug addiction and when it came time to escort him to treatment, his older brother decided to go with him for help with his co-dependency.

I think the key to my success with intervention is that the procedure is flexible (and so am I). The whole job (preparation and presentation and debriefing) is accomplished in stages, usually within a twelve-hour period. That's usually all the time all the participants can coordinate and sustain themselves for together. There is a thing called information overload!

The preparation usually lasts for two to three hours and is done the afternoon before the intervention. Yet, there have been emergency situations and exceptions which may cause the preparation to last little more than an hour and a half before the intervention and may be partly done on the way to the intervention (plane, car, etc.). One time, I intervened on a twenty-year-old woman who was addicted to drugs, and a male friend of hers was excluded from the intervention group because some members of the family didn't want him there. But he came anyway and waited outside. The girl erupted with anger just moments into the intervention and bolted from the room but the friend was there. He had no preparation but spoke from his heart and helped her calm down enough to listen. He had more influence with her than anyone in her family. In another case, our arrangements got mixed up and we ended up convening at a parking lot only minutes before the intervention. My words of wisdom to the participants—"Be sincere, be genuine, give it as gift, and stay with the theme of treatment"—were the only preparation they had. (This is not preferred, yet in an emergency, you adapt due to the severity and the group capability.)

The intervention can last from one to three hours and debriefing is about a half an hour after that. The average intervention with my formula is approximately forty-five minutes long. Other evidence of flexibility is in the fact that the participants (or would-be-if-they-could-be participants) can tape record (audio/video) their messages or write them down in a letter to be read during the intervention. Children, in particular, do well on video. Although tapes and letters can add to the intervention and can be a comfortable means of communicating for some participants, they don't have the same impact as a live presentation. (Back to that idea of the whole group being greater than the sum of the parts it's made of.) Still, a tape or letter can "plant the seed" (of treatment) in the dependent's mind.

MOTIVATIONAL INTERVENTION GOALS

Although the public (including my professional peers) often gauge the success of an intervention by looking at whether or not the addicted person went for treatment immediately, I say the first goal is to present. The patient must be available and have a routine in which an intervention can be planned. If he is available, you're one-third of the way home; if he will sit down, you're two-thirds there; and if he listens—then you've made it home as far as the presentation goes. It may seem like an incidental thing to consider this a goal, but it's far more than a technicality.

When you consider the time and energy that most participants have put forth to prepare and meet for an intervention, it's easy to understand why they have a need to present to the dependent, directly and on time. In other words, they're all pumped up and ready to go! A tremendous amount of energy is fused together for one sudden burst of effectiveness. Waiting around for the dependent who doesn't show up leaves the participants feeling incomplete, drained and exhausted. That combination can provoke anger, resentment, and frustration, totally negating the honorable experience they had assembled for.

The second goal of the group is to motivate the addict to get help—the sooner the better. The participants are prepared to rally for the addict, say and do whatever it takes to motivate them. For example, suppose we're all in a lifeboat, trying to make a bridge out of our arms to reach your loved one who's about to drown in the ocean. If it means a couple of us have to get out of the boat and into the water, so be it. We'll be a team, no matter what it takes. Whether we agree with every little thing or not, whether your loved one fell in the water or jumped in—it doesn't matter. We all got into the lifeboat to save him and one way or another, we'll keep him from drowning. Afterwards, however, if he decides to go back out there, this would be his choice.

Or imagine we're all mountain climbers strung together and your loved one is stranded on a cliff. We are asking him to trust us to swing him over to a safer ledge and pull him up. We're all dedicated to go to the peak today—not tomorrow—and we're not going to allow him to stay stuck on that ledge.

Another goal is that the patient stay in treatment. The intervention procedure is so powerful and meaningful, the patient almost always stays for the full time (approximately three to four weeks or a quality outpatient program). There are times, however, that the person agrees but you seriously doubt they'll stay in treatment. You may think they agreed as a means of concluding the intervention. One time, I intervened on an attorney at his home and five minutes into the intervention he stated, "Okay, I'll go." We were glad, of course, but I had to tell him, "Savor the moment. Here is a group of people who love you so much and care so much about you that they took out time to come and tell you so, themselves. The only time most people get to hear this tribute to themselves is at a funeral. Sit back and enjoy this; it's going to be a very moving experience."

In actuality, very few people ever leave their treatment midway. Part of that success is in the intervention specialist's ability to assess the needs (physical, budgetwise, attitude, status, etc.) of the patient and the family, and the appropriate treatment facility. This is covered in more detail later. I do believe there are certain facilities more appropriate for attracting a patient, i.e., aesthetics, style, etc.

A fourth goal of the group is to help prevent relapse. The intervention is the time when the seed is planted (that life doesn't have to be like this, that there is a solution for the addict). The silence (about the addiction and its side effects) has been broken. Part of what accomplishes this is the fact that once someone is treated, he is never the same. You can't go back—except by conscious choice. The next time the patient is tempted to take a drink or drug, he will remember the group who stood up for him, and the compulsive action will require a new and careful consideration.

Family involvement is also very important to family's continuing recovery from addiction. Additionally, individual/family therapy, anonymous groups, and continued education all help the patient and family prevent a relapse of old thinking by family enablers.

The fifth goal of motivation intervention is the unity of the group. Intervention is a strenuous undertaking for all of the participants. Other issues, opinions, and personality/attitude quirks aside, they all agreed to undertake this one effort to help this person, this one time. They will always be closer for having shared the experience. In fact, what is far more typical than getting people to participate is trying to explain the absence of those you didn't ask. Some people are truly offended at not having been asked.

The unity of the group is paramount to the success of the intervention. There cannot be an atmosphere of unrest in the group. The effect of the people mix has to be uplifting, positive and united in their cause. If there is significant bickering, arguing or other unrest in the group, it may be best to delay the intervention for a period or not utilize this process at all!

SUCCESS STEPS OF THE INTERVENTION

Throughout my research, I've found specific reasons for the success of an intervention. In other words, ask me why this process works, and I'll tell you there are three critical points that must be taken to insure the success of an intervention.

First and foremost is surprise. The prospective patient needs to be taken by surprise, caught off-guard with this bold presentation, this gift of solution for their well-being. This is not a "Judas" act, but a necessary step to create a temporary imbalance of the addict's defenses. In actuality, I've found that the addict is usually relieved, quiet and agreeable—always retaining his/her dignity. It's not as if the person were kidnapped and taken somewhere "for their own good." It's more along the lines of a spontaneous group visit from those who love the person most. It may not be an especially festive occasion, but it's still a happy, powerful surprise.

The surprise takes place anywhere, depending on the circumstances surrounding the loved one. There have been times it has been held in a hospital, at the airport, in a hotel room, at the person's own home, in a car or on a yacht—wherever it can be counted on that the addict will be available and the meeting will be private. The most normal and comfortable setting is the patient's home.

The people-mix or presence is the next step that influences the success of an intervention. One of the easiest ways to imagine an intervention, in terms of the people who participate, is to see the loved one as if he was at his own funeral; the other participants are those who would gather round to honor his life. Who would be the pallbearers, who would give the eulogy? Using the Storti model of intervention, it is critical to have a dedicated, motivating and united group.

Usually, eight to twelve people (though it can be slightly more or less) participate, and it is not limited only to family members. In fact, there is a certain power outsiders carry that goes a long way toward inspiring the dependent. Someone he/she hasn't seen in years can be very inspiring; an old coach or friend from college, or a mentor from years past, often holds more power than the family members do. Another "user" (another alcoholic or person with the same addiction, whether they themselves are recovering or not) is also often helpful. The intervention specialist must monitor this involvement so that the patient doesn't become defensive and see it as a matter of "who's calling the kettle black?" A lot of times, though, a person with the same addiction, someone "coming from the same place" as the addict, is able to appeal to the dependent on equal ground and, thus, their words of encouragement carry more weight. On the other hand, caution must be used with someone who has just been through a treatment center and wants to get his spouse/loved one, etc. to do the same thing. That situation can blow up in your face. Sometimes a person bubbling with the enthusiasm of their newly found recovery can influence the addict the opposite way it is intended. The people mix is very important and the intervention specialist can help the nucleus group in the assessment of the types of people (friends, relatives, clergy, doctor, etc.) that should be considered.

I often include special guests in an intervention as they can reach the addict where the family cannot, for whatever reason. A special guest may be someone with the same addiction, as mentioned before, with a similar background or living circumstances as the patient (someone possibly that the patient doesn't know). It may be someone in the same profession who is in his own recovery, a special friend or old college pal, or a boss or co-worker. These people connect to the addict from a different aspect of the addict's life than the family does and may remind him/her of a part of themselves or their lives that they thought they had lost. It gives them another ray of hope to know they are cared about outside the family. The whole presentation is likened to the Ralph Edwards "This Is Your Life" show, where everyone is present to honor the selected individual by reminding them of their loving history.

Another dimension of the people-mix is the audio/visual presence in an intervention. It is common to have letters of caring and concern from particular relatives and/or friends who would like to participate but couldn't be there in person. In the same vein, audio and video tapes may be presented. These are usually only referred to and shared for a minute or two and then left for the loved one to read or watch or listen to, on his/her own. This is often the best way to include children who are important in the patient's life, too. In one case in which I intervened on an elderly woman, I read excerpts from a letter one of her grandchildren had written and then the woman wanted to hear from the others who had written. She wasn't nearly as impressed with the relatives who were sitting in front of her as she was by the children who had written about their love for her and their hope for her well-being.

The participation of young children in an intervention is an issue that must be considered on a case by case basis. The intervention specialist must gauge the stability of the child and their level of anxiety surrounding the addicted person, as well as their knowledge of the problem. (Usually, this information comes from the parent.) The responsibility for contacting the participants and providing any equipment needed to use audio/visual lies with the core of participants who were part of the assessment.

The third part of making the intervention a success is in the genuineness of the participants. The group normally makes it clear right away that they are there out of love for the addict, that they feel good about participating and would have felt left out otherwise. Humor is allowable when it comes naturally, but not sarcasm or teasing. This is a rescue mission from the heart and everyone must tread lightly. This is not the time to point to things the loved one has done (or not done) or to showcase the consequences of his addiction; these are better left to be discussed in subsequent therapy.

I was quite concerned about this issue in one particular case where we were intervening on a woman alcoholic, because her husband was an engineer. He was very precise and analytical and I hesitated to call upon him for fear he would outline his wife's drunken escapades and the damage she had caused with certain people. But when it came time to hear from him, I will never forget it. The man got up from his chair and knelt

down in front of his wife and said, "I love you, Mari-
anne, and no matter what happens, I will always love
you. And right now, in front of all these people, I want
to rededicate myself to you because you mean everything to me." It was so emotional. All of us were teary-
eyed to witness such a sincere endearment, especially
from one who is normally so rational and unemotional.
That's when I remembered my underlying faith and
spirituality in the intervention process as a whole and
realized how much of it is beyond any of our deliberate
intentions.

In another case, a football coach the patient hadn't
seen for five years was a special guest. He had mentioned that he wanted to memorize something to say
when it was his turn to speak. I was a little reluctant
about this, too, because the key to the presentation is
spontaneity and sincerity of the words each person says
at the time, but eventually I told him it would be all
right. As it turned out, the coach recited a poem about
a man in the glass and being totally honest with one's
self that he and the whole team had learned in training.
It was so touching to see this big, athletic, normally
outspoken man repeating this insightful piece of poetry.
He had never been a man of words, per se, but the
poem had touched his life through sports and he was
able to use it again to touch the life of a young athlete.

This area of being genuine is what the Storti model
cannot provide on its own. There is a "magic," if you
will, a spirituality of the group that transcends the struc-
tures and is actually the guts of the intervention. I am
continually amazed at the simple eloquence of people.

Another tool I have used to help people be able to
put aside their anger or hostility toward the addict and

get into the mood of being more inspirational and motivational than accusatory and negative is to have them imagine I am a physician who has just given them the news that the patient has only a short while (maybe an hour) to live. From this perspective I would ask, "What do you want to say to this person?" This is not an attempt to excuse or gloss over what the addict may have done or said that has been hurtful to others—this is just not the time to discuss it. The time will come in therapy, in treatment or learning to detach with love.

Contingency Plan

Another segment of the intervention process that runs parallel to the intervention itself is creating a contingency plan. The immediate family must have a work-plan for themselves, must be open to their own changes, and must set new boundaries. That's not to say they have to disown the addict or threaten to terminate any ties to them, but part of the reason the initial inquiry was made about an intervention is because the family is at its wit's end. It can no longer function as it has been.

Once the intervention has been held, the secret is out—there's no turning back for anyone. With the patient accepting help, the immediate family is to follow through with family treatment. A change in the whole family has already occurred. The contingency plan is a means of helping the change remain a positive one, and it requires the whole family's commitment to involvement which may range from continued open discussion, to reading self-help books, to attendance at anonymous groups, to individual/family therapy, to specific acts of "tough love." Just as the intervention is not a way to pin all the (family) trouble on one person's addiction, the contingency plan doesn't leave recovery completely in the hands of the individual at the treatment center. Many issues and lots of internal, emotional work is yet to be done and the contingency plan recognizes that work. It is the rest of the family's self-contract for progress. Now is the time to work your own plan.

It's also important for the participating group to stay unified in their efforts to be supportive. That means not segregating the family into small cliques—even if it's only for this one issue (of the loved one's addiction) that you're united, you must stick together about it afterwards. It also means not downplaying the importance of the intervention once it's over, not referring to it in jest, and not defending it. Remember, you gave the intervention as an honorable gift—you can't ridicule it or try to justify it later without damaging its effectiveness.

Consequences are another part of the contingency plan in that there will be corresponding reaction (from the dependent) to every consequence threatened in the intervention. This is often referred to as leverage—"Go to treatment now or I'm getting a divorce." "You check into the treatment center today, or you don't set foot in this house again." Consequences or leverage thrown at the addicted loved one can sour an intervention very quickly. My method doesn't use the "or else" tool, although some professional therapists thrive on its role in the intervention (and it becomes the norm rather than the exception). There can be a time or place for this, but I believe this kind of statement is just asking for trouble; for one thing, the family very often cannot live up to what they say. They are sending mixed messages. Their new resolve will melt with time and the love they truly feel for the individual will get lost again in the revolving continuance of the patient and family habits being normal.

Another reason leverage seldom works is that addicts are often addicted to a double-edged sword—there is an excitement at the thought of doing the opposite deed and proving that you're wrong. Consequences leave a bad taste in the mouth because it changes the intervention into a form of punishment and ridicule, rather than a gift of the heart. Pride is the other major issue when confronting the loved one with a "you will or else—" statement. The patient feels compelled to take the "or else." Unfortunately, despite the knowledge of this typical reaction to threatening consequences, 90 percent of professionals still maintain leverage is a critical part of the intervention. "You have to be willing to put your marriage on the line." "Of course, you have to accept the idea of kicking your daughter out of your house and not accepting phone calls from her and not helping her for x amount of time—forever, if need be." These are very harsh and drastic measures that have no place in the Storti model of intervention. These are not messages from one heart to another. It has occurred during the intervention that certain family announced future boundaries, but to state lines of separation is to create animosity.

There are four basic reasons why proposing certain consequences should be given very careful consideration. One of these is the time element. People will wait (sometimes for years) before feeling ready to put their marriage or other relationship on the line. They don't need to wait and suffer for all that time. I have had people inquire about an intervention on their spouse and when I explain how gentle the process is designed to be handled, they say, "You mean I don't have to be ready to divorce him? Why did I wait fifteen years to call you?" Somewhere down the road, someone told them they had to have strong leverage or wait until the person bottoms out. Neither issue is true and it's truly a shame that so many people live in such pain in and around addiction because of common misconceptions such as these. If you don't get anything else out of this book, get this: Motivational intervention is one procedure that is an option for your consideration. You may not do it immediately. It may not even be right for you and yours at all, but you owe it to yourself to consider the possibility. Talk to a few intervention specialists and get different opinions.

A second aspect of consequences that needs to be weighed carefully is the dichotomy between love and leverage. Punishment often leads to negative feelings. It doesn't make sense to say, "We love you but if you don't get help, we're going to do such-and-such." (Employers and teens are exceptions; sometimes this approach may be appropriate for them.)

Also, if you threaten certain consequences, you must be prepared to carry them out. Otherwise, you lose all credibility with the addict and you defeat the plans you made for yourself. Pride and leverage are not compatible, and by using leverage you confront the addict's pride.

Thirdly, you must keep in mind the reality of delayed reactions. Part of the purpose of the intervention is to "plant the seed" that there is hope of a better way to live than in the vicious cycles of addiction. There is hope. The reality of the delayed reaction is that even without a word said, when the intervention stage is set, the seed is planted and you must allow time for it to take root. Think of it as if you had a loved one who has just had surgery. The doctor comes out of the surgery room and tells you the patient is in recovery, the surgery went well, but we'll just have to wait and see, right now. We have to be patient and let the loved one accept the surgical repair. In one case I worked on, six of us had met at a hotel in Colorado where the addict was expected to come for a business conference. He never showed. Someone had tipped him off about the intervention and he opted to leave the state. Was the intervention a failure? No. With only the thought of it, the seed was planted. Thirteen months later, the man checked himself into the treatment center we had planned to offer that day.

Everyone will be changed (however slightly) by participating in the intervention, and the addict will be most changed. He or she will not be able to sustain his/her addiction with quite the same ease as he/she did before. The intervention shatters some illusions the addict may have about his/her anonymity, his/her power and even his/her worth (ego)—they can't turn their backs on that knowledge once it's declared publicly.

In my experience there is no failed intervention. In those cases where the addict did not agree to go for treatment immediately, I've found that anywhere from twenty-four hours to a year and a half later, the message got through and they went themselves. The seed that had been planted took root. Be patient and remember, your decisions don't have to depend on whether or not the person goes to treatment.

Self-abuse is the fourth reason you must be very careful about waging consequences. Addicts are often addicted to self-abuse and self-imposed punishment and they may even dare someone to present some leverage. It's as if he/she needs the possible pain to survive. In the Storti model of intervention, total withdrawal of the family from a loved one is never recommended. It's too unlikely it could be (or should be) maintained. However, new or tighter boundaries are often recommended—for everyone's health. This is particularly true with teenagers. Another kind of boundary that can work well in certain circumstances is the employer saying to the addict, "If you go for treatment, we can keep your job for you. If you don't, we can't keep you on because your addiction is affecting your work."

Whether any kind of leverage is used or not, everyone should remember the power words have—they can inspire and they can scar a person. We want to love them into treatment.

VIGNETTE—ENOUGH IS ENOUGH

It seemed as if the day would never end; appointments all day and the commute home on the infamous Southern California freeway system cost me an extra hour tonight. I barely had time to grab a bite to eat, kick off my shoes and catch the end of the news on television before I prepared to make a conference call from my home.

I quickly reviewed my notes from a conversation I had had yesterday with a young woman named Cindy.

She had called me on behalf of her thirty-nine-year-old brother. Tonight we would talk with their parents, Pat and Lisa, and a cousin named Alex. Cindy told me yesterday that the whole family and her brother's supervisor at work were worried about Gerry. He was addicted to alcohol, writing bad checks and spending money excessively. He was recently divorced and lived close to his two children, who were seven and nine years of age.

The family lived in New York, only one generation removed from their relatives who immigrated to America from one of the Scandinavian countries. I needed to get a feeling for the physical and psychological stability of both Gerry and the rest of the family to determine if an intervention would help them or not. I knew Gerry was out of his job temporarily, on a medical disability for stress, but Cindy hadn't told me he was also addicted to pornography, sex and even cross-dressing. He would purchase new clothes from the finer stores in town and tell the store clerk they were for his wife, charging the expense on a credit card or writing bad checks for them. But he was so guilt-ridden about the cross-dressing, he would wear them once and then burn them and have to repurchase everything for the next time.

Even over the phone, I could tell the parents were having a great deal of difficulty just admitting to these truths—especially to a stranger. I explained the risks involved in doing an intervention and that was when Lisa, Gerry's mother, broke down and left Pat on the phone with Alex and myself. She came back on a few minutes later.

Upon further discussion, I decided an intervention

could be very helpful in this situation. The hardest part of the case from a professional standpoint, however, was deciding on a particular diagnosis to address during the intervention. Typically, you give the gift of treatment to someone in answer to his/her addiction, but in this case, Gerry had so many addictions, it was difficult to tell which one was predominant. This is also a sensitive area for the intervention specialist, for the addict may be willing to acknowledge only one particular addiction.

We decided to cite his addiction to alcohol and cocaine as a trend in excessiveness that leads him to extreme impulsive behavior. We also wanted to be careful not to expose Gerry's activities to his employer because we weren't sure how much he knew about the other excessive behavior and sensitivity, keeping in mind that, once in treatment, more will be revealed. We set a date for next Tuesday; I would fly into La Guardia Airport Monday to prepare the family.

It sounded normal enough, but as it turned out, that weekend had started one of the worst storms New York had seen in four years and, of course, coming from the Golden State, my overcoat was as close as I could get to winter attire. It was a late flight made longer and longer due to circling the airport waiting for the runway to be cleared for landing. I made it to the hotel only to find there had been an error and my room had been given to someone else. (Since the weather had delayed so many flights, the hotel was now booked to capacity.) I was starving and tired and frozen and not my usual cheerful self. Eventually, I got a room—or rather, a closet. It must have been a hideaway room for one of the employees but it had a bed and blankets and once

I resigned myself to the fact that there were no coffee shops or snack bars or restaurants open anywhere within walking distance, I decided it would do just fine.

The next day, Gerry's employer, Mark, picked me up and we went to the parents' home to prepare. It never ceases to impress me how much courage the average person has when they're called on. The whole family was scared; they were a proud and stoic breed. Survivors all the way. But most of all, they were a family. They cared for each other deeply. As Gerry's brother said, "No matter what, he's our brother. He's in trouble—quicksand of a sort. The way I see it, 'treatment' is a 'treat' we want to give him to help himself. Disease means he is ill at ease; he is suffering!"

I couldn't have said it better myself. The preparation was long and involved and I was duly weary when I returned to the hotel. The next morning, I awakened renewed and excited to get on with the intervention—feeling warm and rested and fed, and looking forward to the blast of cold air that would greet me en route to meet the parents. My enthusiasm for January mornings in New York lasted about two seconds. It was five degrees below zero and windy.

"L-l-l-l-l-let's just get going," I told the others, my teeth chattering between every couple of words, "before I freeze to death." They laughed and you might say the "ice was broken." "W.W.B.D.!" I rallied. "We won't be denied!"

We walked into Gerry's house and were hit with a thick, musty wall of cigarette smoke that enveloped the whole house in a musty dinginess. Everything had a distinctly unsavory feel to it; I had a hard time breathing but I couldn't tell if it was the smoke or the very atmosphere that made me nervous.

Gerry at the floor, straight-backed and Indian-style. He smoked calmly, but with an eerie presence, as if he had secret forces he could summon from beneath the floor or in the walls, if need be. He listened silently but with detachment, as in déjà vu. He had expected this. Not today, but somehow, he seemed to have known this moment would come. He listened to everyone—his parents, sister Cindy, his college friend Larry, his boss and cousin and myself, and he agreed with the idea but had a lot of things that would need to be worked out before he could actually go.

The parents spoke from their hearts and everyone could feel the love for Gerry through their difficulty in speaking out. Once, when Gerry turned sharply at something his father mentioned, Lisa, his mother, broke down and sobbed, fearful of the possible violence to follow. But Gerry resumed his posture and got back into his trance-like mode.

"I have to finish the Ximeter Project at work and prepare for the orientation for the corporate office next month," Gerry said after all his other objections had been handled by one person or another. Part of the preparation is anticipating the addict's objections and assigning people to take care of whatever tasks are necessary.

"It will all be taken care of, Gerry," his boss said. "I'd like you to consider treatment to be your new assignment. You are a valued employee we depend on for some of our most important work and we don't want to lose you. Your condition is affecting your work and we are ready to support you right now in getting the proper treatment. Your job will be waiting for you."

Gerry acquiesced. "I want to see my kids first," he said. They lived only a few miles away so we decided Cindy and Mark would take him on the way to the airport en route to the treatment center. The parents followed their car to the house where the kids lived and I watched him squat down and put his big arms around them as they huddled on the sidewalk in private discussion. We then drove on to the airport; I remember how peaceful I felt looking through the windshield at the road ahead. The whole scene, road and fields alike glistened under the new fallen snow that crisp January morning. The storm had passed. Soon they would begin to shovel the roads and get everything circulating again. But for now, it was so serene.

Both parents told me how relieved they felt at having participated in the intervention today; so much had gone unspoken, unrecognized, for so long. Before the meeting, we had taken an informal poll amongst ourselves, guessing the odds of Gerry going to treatment. They said they saw a 40 percent chance that he would go, and only 20 percent that he would stay for the full term—not quite the confidence level I like to have behind me going into an intervention.

"Well, whether he goes or stays or not," the mother said, "this is the best thing we could have done. We've done all that we can and he knows how much we all care about him, for sure. Everything's out in the open."

"It's up to him, now," Gerry's father said in agreement.

"Savor the moment, folks," I advised them as they dropped me off at the airport. "This is a wonderful thing you've all done; the future will come soon enough." I left and checked in my baggage. All the flights were delayed because of the cold and snow, and my plane wasn't due to leave for three hours anyway, so I walked over to the gate Gerry would be leaving from. His plane was scheduled to take off in forty-five minutes. I started to panic when there were only twenty minutes before boarding and they hadn't shown up. What had happened? Cindy was driving, or did Gerry refuse to get back into the car after he spoke to his kids? The employer was with them—surely he would have been able to carry out the escort, wouldn't he? The door was opened behind the ticket desk now and the airline called for its first passengers. I kept pacing back and forth, hoping to catch the trio running toward the gate, ticket in hand. The lump in my throat sunk to my stomach and settled heavily. I should have ridden with them. Why didn't I ask the parents to wait and follow them every inch of the way?

"Last call for Flight No. 486 to—" I heard over the loudspeaker. This was it! After all that talk, all the ordeal of the entire preparation and intervention—after all that, nothing. He wasn't even going to make it to the plane! Feeling terribly responsible, I called the parents.

"I don't want to alarm you, Lisa," I told his mother, "but I'm at the gate Gerry was supposed to leave from and they haven't come. The plane is getting ready to take off. I don't know what's happening." We hung up and I remembered the irony of how I had just told them less than an hour ago to savor the moment because you never know how long it would last.

I went back over to the window by the gate. They were de-icing the plane—spraying it with a syrupy,

Pepto-Bismol–like substance. I could use something for my own stomach at this point. Just as I turned to go over to my gate area, I saw the three of them rushing to the ticket desk. They were laughing! The stewardess called the pilot and instructed him not to let the jetway tunnel to the door of the plane be extracted just yet and someone opened the other side and whisked Gerry and Mark onto the plane.

"He wanted to stop for a couple of beers, for lunch," Cindy informed me. "Said if he was going to go into treatment today, and he didn't want to drink on the plane, he needed a couple of belts before he left. And we went along."

Alas, I could breathe again.

I heard from Cindy a year or so later and she reported her brother had stayed for the full four-week treatment and then extended it an additional six months, as there were so many issues to deal with. I was glad to be part of the intervention that led Gerry to such dedication to his own recovery.

The Only Failure Is the Failure to Act

Intervention is not for everyone, but it is an option that is available and should be considered. Each situation has to be assessed on its own, however, and many consider it to be the last thing they can try to bring their loved one back into harmony with life. Actually, the family owes itself considering an intervention—just to know that they did everything they could for their loved one, as well as for themselves. Even if the addict will not sit down and listen to the presentation, even if they panic or get angry and bolt out of the room, the presence of the people will have made a statement and a seed will have been planted. This truth is evidenced by the small number of people who refuse to sit through an intervention and find themselves checking into a treatment center on their own weeks or months later.

Remember, too, that it doesn't hurt to ask, and by reading this book you will already be more informed than most about the whole intervention process. Your next step will be to contact a professional intervention specialist and inquire about his techniques and procedures.

THE INQUIRY

Generally, the inquiry takes between fifteen and thirty minutes: however, getting up the nerve to make the first call may take years. I remember once hearing an admission intake counselor say to someone who called for the first time, "Congratulations for your courage in making this first call," and I thought how nice that was and appropriate. People are afraid to call and it does take courage to do it in spite of their fear. We in the profession of addictive disease can never forget the fright of someone making that first call; whether it is the addicted person or a co-dependent, the fear is tremendous.

The inquiry call is made to tell the specialist what the situation is, what kind of help the family requests, and why they need it. For example, a man may call and say, "My wife is an alcoholic; she's tried to stop on her own, and I've tried everything from anonymous groups to threatening to divorce her. I don't know what else to do. I travel a lot, and I'm afraid to leave her with the kids because she gets so mean. She's been in the hospital twice from car accidents she had while driving drunk. Do you think you can help, or what can you offer?"

The type of addiction is identified as well as the danger that surrounds the addiction and the type of behavior the caller is concerned about. At the same time, the intervention specialist needs to get a feel for the contact person. How serious is the situation? Is there other action the person can take first? The specialist offers hope and makes referrals when an intervention doesn't seem to be the best route to take.

Only forty of every one hundred inquiries actually matures to an intervention. There are several reasons for this, the primary one being that the family is not ready. An intervention is stressful for everyone—a fear of the unknown is there, worry about the addict, or his behavior, hovers overhead, and the sheer logistics of staging an intervention and coordinating all the participants for the event can be a big burden. The family must be unified in their concern and in their support of the intervention idea—if there is bickering or other disharmony among the family members, the intervention may not be feasible at this time. Another reason a specialist may recommend not having an intervention is that the case is too explosive. The addict may have a habit of going into a violent rage when confronted with his addiction or the family members may be so consumed with (years of) anger that they are prone to volatile action themselves. Another reason interventions are postponed or recommended against is that no funds are available to send the addict to a treatment center. Traditionally, the treatment is part of the gift the group is giving the addict, which means they pool their resources to finance the loved one's inpatient or outpatient treatment. Depending on the circumstances and the insurance coverage, this is a major hurdle for many families.

THE ASSESSMENT

If the inquiry leads toward the possibility of an intervention, assessing the situation in more detail is necessary to support the inquirer's statements about the addiction, the trouble the addicted person is in, and how the rest of the family is situated. The actual assessment may be a conference call held with three people or an appointment between the specialist and the contact person with a few other family members. It's often helpful to have a relative in the assessment to play "devil's advocate" and bring out all the negative possibilities that might occur if they go forward with the intervention, or someone to help shoulder some responsibility of the decision to go forward.

The assessment can be a frightening experience to many; some people feel they are being disloyal, others feel guilty about talking behind their loved one's back, and yet others feel the whole process is somewhat of a secretive, cloak-and-dagger endeavor. A sensitive specialist will ease the people through the discussion gently while asking questions about the addict's living situation. This is the point at which the intervention specialist must gauge the difficulty of the case based on the physical health, job, social patterns of the dependent, then decide whether or not the intervention is feasible and wise. Other things that must be discussed are the primary diagnosis or dysfunction that will be named in the intervention, family dynamics, who else will be asked (or not asked) to participate, and aftercare.

The assessment is a private interview that may last two to three hours for the family and the intervention specialist. The family needs to be informed about the risk factors involved in an intervention, the surprise element (the addict has no knowledge of and does not come to the assessment), red flags, contingency plans, the genuineness that must be conveyed, and the input the specialist can expect from the family during the intervention. The stabilization of the nucleus of the family group varies: from those who are confident among themselves that they can motivate the addict to those who are almost afraid of even being at the assessment. The extent of the specialist's input will correspond directly with how much "hand-holding" he must do with the family.

In short, it's an intervention orientation—a brief overview of the entire process, its goals and intentions and the basic procedures. It is usually a case of "information overload" to the small group that comes to the assessment. In fact, this book could be a major portion of the assessment, the other parts being the personalization the specialist must give for the specific circumstances and profiling the pathology or problem and the proper treatment solution. Once the people understand the basic idea of motivational intervention and what it entails, they are ready to interview different intervention professionals to see the particular specialty and personality each brings to the situation.

THE PREPARATION

If the family decides to proceed with the intervention, the next step is their preparation. This is a two or three

hour meeting between them and the intervention specialist where the goals and procedures are clearly speci-
fied—what the family members should or should not
say, when and where the intervention will be held, how
the joint arrival of everyone will be handled, who will
escort the addict, etc. Other details, such as what to
do about phones, TV, pets, restrooms, etc., are also
discussed during the preparation.

This is a tough time for the intervention specialist as
it is where he must exceed the family's/friends' expectations and build their confidence in the whole idea of the
intervention. This is when the specialist instills positive
energy in the unified effort of the family. It is also the
time when the specialist can memorize the names of
the family members, work out the case in his mind
to the order in which to call on the participants and
recommend what they should say or not say. The intervention specialist has to go through this process with
each family so it is fairly routine to him, but because it
is a new and (possibly) frightful experience for the family, he must take time to explain everything completely.
Often, the specialist will also ask the immediate family
members to write down particular reasons why the patient needs treatment. These examples are normally
passed on to the treatment therapist for later reference.
Most interventions never even get into discussions
about the specific reasons for getting help; by that point,
it's usually already an accepted premise by the participants and the patient. (Why stay in the problem? Let's
get into the solution.) Most preparations are done in
someone's home, office, hotel suite, etc., where it is
quiet and private and the process is fully talked out.
The group normally leaves wishing they could just

drive over and do the intervention immediately (which has occurred in some instances).

INTERVENTION FORMULA

The Storti method of intervention is so successful because of its heart to heart approach in making the presentation a positive conversation. The participants give every reason they can think of that shows why the addict is loved and respected and cared about and then offer a solution of treatment that will work.

This is when you stand up for this loved one. It's not meant to be tattletale time, when you say, "Look what you've done!" It's a tribute, a loving roast, a eulogy of sorts that says, "Here's what you're all about. You're such a good person and we love you. We don't want to lose you—let us help you to help yourself." It's a highly inspirational presentation that often leaves everyone (myself included) a little teary-eyed with compassion. The emotional genuineness runs over like water over the tiers of a fountain. It's a moment of endearment, of general concern—a snapshot of "I love you-ism." Ninety percent of interventions stay in this stage of the group talk while the specialist highlights the positive aspects of treatment.

Using certain specifics in the intervention is a part of the formula that must be handled very carefully. Quite frankly, the specifics are rarely ever needed. Pointing out evidence of the addict's distinctive behavior under the influence will change the whole feel of the intervention. Those examples should only be used when the addict refuses to accept his need for treatment or is extremely vague in accepting that he has a problem. The intervention specialist must be sensitive to how much the addict can take and walks a very thin tight-rope between making his point as well as the others without sounding condescending and punitive. There are times when I have not used this phase when the patient has been on the verge of wanting to leave the session. It can be aborted and not used at all.

Another important part of the intervention formula is each participant's concern for himself or herself. If the patient will not accept the solution, there is a time in the intervention that this phase is appropriate for the group to end with dignity, yet express their own concerns about the future. Part of the reason for having an intervention in the first place is to answer the help-lessness of the family. They can't go on living with this addiction as they have been—not only is the dependent in pain, so are they. They are all spinning around to-gether in the squirrel cage. A case in point is a recent one in which we had fifteen participants and the patient fully agreed to treatment. Afterwards, the brother of the patient said, "Ed, it's just amazing how many peo-ple the addict affects." And it's true for all of us. Ad-dicted to a substance or not, we are all pebbles that ripple outward to the whole pond.

The intervention must hold some solution for the family as well as the addict. It has to draw a line in the time of the family that says, "From this day forward—I must get some help for myself, while you deal with your addiction in whatever way you must."

A young woman named Lisa said it well when we intervened on her father. She said, "Dad, I'll always love you. You mean everything to me and I appreciate all the things you've given me over the years—my val-ues, my education, vacations, everything. Today, I felt a responsibility to give you this gift of treatment and I'm real disappointed that you won't accept it. I still love you and I'll still be with you for visiting and phone calls and football games, but I won't discuss treatment again. And today, I'm going to get help for me. I hope that for yourself you reconsider, but starting today, it's not my responsibility. It is yours! I'm free from the bondage of thinking, I should have done something. I now know I've tried everything I could."

That's how my method of intervention works—it offers the addict a solution and sets free the intimate family members. It's scary for everyone, and some people think they're being protective by not participating, but, in truth, you can be so protective that you're destructive. It brings out the positive aspects of a person's life and activities and then overwhelms them with love and compassion. The negatives will come out soon enough in treatment and will be handled with the family in the right environment. The intervention is not the time or the place for them.

FOLLOW-UP

What happens after the intervention? When the addict has agreed to go to treatment, the preassigned escorts help him pack, and take him to the treatment center or the airport, if it's out of state. When the escort team has whisked away the addict, the intervention specialist debriefs the family. This is when we all breathe a sigh of relief and relax in the knowledge that we did the best we could. I caution everyone to savor this moment because none of us knows what the future may bring. I've not had the experience of an addicted person not going in for treatment once they have agreed to go. Most people stay for the full treatment, but some have left earlier than the clinicians recommended. Whether the addict makes it to treatment or stays in it as prescribed and whether or not he continues recovery efforts, the family can feel proud and confident that they did this honorable presentation for their loved one. Now they can release the responsibility—not completely, but a great deal more than they ever could have individually. In one case in which we intervened on a man in his forties, suffering with alcoholism, he walked out of the intervention, refusing to go to treatment. Six months later, his wife called and said the man had rolled his truck in an auto accident and was now paralyzed from the neck down. She said she and her daughter were so glad that they had tried to help him through an intervention. They felt that they had done all that they could—the fact that he wouldn't accept their gift was his decision. As sorry as she was for her husband's pain, she suffered no guilt about it.

The intervention specialist handles pre-admission and coordinates with the treatment center to make sure someone will meet the escort group. He gives a verbal evaluation of the intervention and identifies specific issues for the therapist who will be assigned to the patient and forwards a written evaluation and/or specific memos about the intervention. The intervention specialist is normally the liaison between the patient and the family, through the therapist. However, the patient can sometimes block the path by refusing to sign a release of information notice. Typically, for the first week, I make five to six calls to the treatment center and therapist and to the family to make sure all is going well.

Because of the heavy caseloads, most of the reports back to me from the therapist/case manager are weekly, verbal updates.

The intervention specialist generally fades out of the picture after that, as the treatment starts to gel. There certainly can be a delayed reaction by the patient. As he goes through treatment, he begins to have some new feelings about the intervention process. The intervention is kind of like getting into the heart by laser and then getting out. The laser didn't hurt, but afterwards, the patient oozes with pain and possibly misunderstandings or he grieves. Letters of endearment given by all in attendance sure help out. The start of treatment can be lonely, serious and awkward. In other words, you can feel very "raw" and minimize why you are even in treatment or make phones calls to certain members of the group to make them feel they made a mistake. However, once the patient is in full treatment, he starts to relate and bond with his peers. We must also remember the spouse or co-dependent goes through this rollercoaster of emotions and also needs support. That's why the group is to unify and not create different camps—they must support the family and stay confident with the patient about the need to have intervened.

Personally, I take pride in doing a thorough follow-up. In fact, as an example, I recently received this note from one of the people I worked with on an intervention. "Your follow-up was wonderful. I felt as if I were your only client. I was very impressed by your personal attention. I hope other intervention specialists strive for this type of follow-up."

Vignette—Sex in Seven Minutes

I was taking a twenty-minute breather between appointments on a late Tuesday afternoon when I got the inquiry from Gina.

"It's my brother," she told me, with a resolve I could tell she'd spent all day working up to. "He's an alcoholic and also uses crystal meth. His life is totally unmanageable and he's draining my mom, emotionally and financially. He's been arrested twice. We have to do something!"

"How old is he?" I asked.

"He's thirty-eight and his name is Otis."

"Does he work?"

"No," Gina said, before taking a deep breath in which to spill the rest of the story about how Otis had managed to sustain a physical injury on the job over two years ago and now lives primarily off disability insurance. "His health has deteriorated and it shows; he does okay for short periods of time, but then he falls back again."

We spoke for a little while longer and arranged a conference call between Gina and her husband, Lance, myself, and Otis's mother, Hilda. Eventually, I took the case and flew to Phoenix, Arizona, to do the intervention. One thing about doing the conference call, though, is that I often don't ask the people I'm speaking to how I might recognize them at the airport. It's a little game I like to play to test my perception and observation skills.

It felt good to stand up again as I reached into the overhead compartment for my suit jacket and briefcase.

I walked out into the dry, hot sun that kept the temperature in the low hundreds. I looked around as I approached the inside of the airport and noticed two eager, but strained, faces watching for this stranger they summoned to help their loved one.

Lance and Gina drove me to Hilda's house in a nice, air-conditioned luxury car. It was pleasant talking to them. They were both career professionals, calm and kind, with a good sense of humor. They made me feel that I fit in. I wasn't hot anymore, I wasn't crowded and stiff; I was ready to go do work, ready to prepare this caring family to present to Otis. What I wasn't ready for was Monique.

She looked like a discarded girlfriend of Hell's Angels, wearing a tight, stained and ragged T-shirt and cut-offs with leather sandals and carrying her painted denim jacket over her shoulder. She didn't need the jacket for the climate but for status. What status? I wasn't sure if her dark, reddish-brown hair was tangled inadvertently or if she had teased it mercilessly, but the tattoos that spiraled down around the whole length of her arm were obviously deliberate. She wore chains for necklaces and her knobby hands sported chunky silver men's rings. Suddenly, I got a whole different impression of Otis, although all of them assured me he was not prone to violence.

"He's just a little—" Gina warned.

"Bizarre?" Lance filled in.

"Eccentric is a better work, I think," she said.

"Hmph!" Lance replied, doing nothing further to contradict his wife. I wondered what I had gotten myself into this time. Forget the semantics—are you sure we should do this, I asked myself. It's part of my job to lead the pep rally and get the others enthused and feeling mighty enough to brave the challenge; that's hard to do when you're thinking of running scared yourself. But we all forged ahead as I prepared the family and girlfriend for tomorrow's meeting.

The next morning was bright and warm, even at 8 A.M. In fact, the temperature hadn't dropped below 75 degrees last night. We met as planned in the parking lot of a department store and rode over to Otis's house in two cars—Lance and Gina in one and myself, Monique and Hilda in the other. We made a path across a front lawn strewn with Harley Davidson motorcycles to the front doorstep.

Monique entered the house first and after pushing some others out of the living room invited us in while she went upstairs to get Otis. Any personal biases I held about rowdy bikers were now melted together with my prejudice against drug dealers, as I was about smothered with a horrendous smell from the kitchen. It certainly wasn't a recipe from the Betty Crocker's Best Cookbook that they were preparing. Just a minute or so later, Otis walked down the stairs and as he refused to shake hands with me until he washed them, I felt my drug suspicions were confirmed.

Otis was a big guy (aren't all the Hell's Angels?)—looking as mangy and dirty as if he'd been living in the same pair of jeans for the past month, riding through the desert with no access to water. He was unshaven, with a tanned complexion and long, knotted, dark brown hair that further darkened his features, which only accentuated his spookiness. Still, he was quiet and he listened.

We spoke for about ten minutes when suddenly he

got up and left the room. He came back with a six-pack of beer to set on his lap and flipped open a can with the pop-top, obviously settling in to listen to what we had come to say. I could see him respond to the gentleness his family offered, despite his rough exterior. He laughed and joked around at inappropriate times, yet he eventually accepted and agreed to go to treatment. Honestly, I was absolutely shocked!

While Otis and Monique went upstairs to pack, the family asked me to help escort him. The thought of a two-hour drive across the desert with this eerie, unkempt, biking free spirit (as Gina referred to him) was truly frightening. The man would change face in an instant, altering his mood and the atmosphere of everyone around him, from a quiet, slightly-weird-but-nice guy to this strapping, sardonic and menacing rebel about to get even with society by one final act of rage. Still, I agreed to go with them.

While they were packing, Monique touched my elbow slightly and motioned me to the bottom of the stairs.

"He'll be gone about three to four weeks, you say?" she asked.

"Yes."

"Well," she said, raising her eyebrows slightly (but with no trace of humor). "We'd like to 'bond' first. Tricia, and the two of us," she said, alluding to a much younger girl sitting half-dressed at the top of the stairs. It was daytime, the hall light wasn't on, and I really didn't want to know about her anyway. I turned my attention back to Monique who was still speaking as if we had always been on the same wavelength. "You understand—one quick fling before he goes," about their request for time out to bond.

Feeling my professional credibility as the omniscient "doctor" was at stake, I nodded. "Of course—well, about how long will this take."

With nary a blink of her eye, Monique replied, "Seven minutes." They must have had the sexual ritual down to a science, but I was embarrassed enough without asking for any more details. His mother wasn't though.

"What are they doing up there?" she asked me after the rumble of the ceiling had caught her attention.

In the end, we did set out for the treatment center. Gina drove and I sat up front with her while Lance rode in the back seat with Otis. With Otis as erratic as he was in the car, the length of the drive seemed like an eternity to me. He brought all of his toys (not the girls) with him—alcohol, drugs, and a porn film. He was imagining something akin to Club Med and it took a constant, heavy concentration to redirect him to the reality of a treatment center that I knew he would actually meet. He went through the program and, later on, slipped into a relapse. But it was different this time (as it always is after an intervention); the seed had been planted and he looked at himself with honesty and checked himself back into treatment again and is doing very well now. I never did follow up on Monique and their ways of bonding, however.

The Cutting Edge

S taging a motivational intervention can be likened to surgery in many respects, particularly in that it is a delicate procedure orchestrated by a specialist and is usually pursued in a last-hope effort to save the patient. Previous prescriptions have not helped to the extent needed; it's time to interrupt destiny!

With an objective for the intervention to be a loving, caring presentation, the initial incision (the start) must be done very carefully so as not to open up any bigger part of the wound than is absolutely necessary. Over time, I have fortunately been able to refine this skill, using a low tone of voice, speaking smoothly and calmly while conveying the honor of the moment.

The point of surgery is a moment of emergency whereby the family and intervention specialist have recognized the patient's condition as a life-death situation.

"Now" is the time zone and we must get the patient to see that urgency as well.

Verbally, the incision (the start of the intervention) serves to anesthetize the patient, sedating him or her to the point that the patient will (mentally) uncross his arms and stay open to what is being said. Yet, the words must be sharp enough to keep the patient's attention; you can't afford to have his/her mind wandering. Sometimes, this requires a certain amount of flair or entertaining on the part of the intervention specialist and the group—theatrics to maintain the crisis zone consciousness. If the intervention is too dull, the patient will take over the presentation.

It's a powerful and awkward time for everyone present, especially the patient. It's as if he/she were lying on the gurney under the hot, bright lights in the operating room, only partially aware of what's going on, and he sees a handful of the most important people in his life standing around him, ready to assist the surgeon. They surround him like a team fully committed to doing their job and fully confident that the surgeon is leading them in exactly the right direction. With all those who love him standing there, ready to assist, the patient is usually calmed and that much more willing to accept the pain and the risk of unknown factors of the operation. For, if all these people who truly love him and have his best interests at heart believe that this is right, it must be so. It may sound naive and is surely simplistic, but there is a real power in the group even before they begin to actually say a word in the intervention. They unconsciously validate the specialist's solution just by their presence—give him credibility and encouragement like a silent team of cheerleaders shouting, "Yes! Yes! This is the way!"

This truth of the power in the group standing behind the specialist was clearly evident in one of my cases in which the patient (and most all of the participants) were Japanese. There was an obvious language and cultural barrier that could not have been transcended without the presence of the group. One of the participants said it to me most clearly: "We are empowering you and your solution," he said. "You cannot convince our brother on your own but we give you credibility by standing beside you. He rests in the knowledge that those who love him most agree that this answer you present is the right course of action." It was true—my words, my technique and my expertise would not carry me without the unified influence of the family and friends the patient respected.

In another case, I intervened on a man who was an alcoholic, and one of the participants later pointed out the power of the group. The intervention was presented in the man's apartment, which happened to have been my wife's and my first apartment house after we had gotten married, some twenty-five years ago. The couple lived only two apartments from where we lived. The man agreed to go to treatment fairly quickly, and while he was preparing to go, his son-in-law came up to congratulate me.

"Good job," he said. "You obviously love what you're doing."

"I do, and it's a privilege," I started to explain, when he interrupted me."

"I'm a salesman, you know," he said, and I go in cold to the buyer. The one thing you've got going for you is that you have a ready reserve of credibility with you at the time of your sales presentation. If I had Mom and a sister or brother and a couple of friends agreeing with me and standing with the client while I was pitching a sale, no way could I miss!"

That's how effective the group presence is. Just being there says so much to the patient, and that's how the stage is set for surgery. Typically, the intervention begins when the patient comes into the room and is greeted with the hugs and kisses that usually accompany any surprise gift. The intervention specialist introduces himself and their purpose there, speaking for the group. This is the very beginning of the incision, when the scalpel just touches the skin. The specialist reassures the patient that this is a presentation to honor him, and thereby begins laying the cards on the table with tender honesty and loving words. It is up to the intervention specialist to direct or choreograph the operation by calling on others and interweaving their words, using them like surgical tools to appeal to the heart of the patient, rather than the mind. Since most people caught in an addictive disease have numbed their feelings for so long, this approach literally cuts through to the heart and they usually well up with tears.

Not long ago, I had a similar experience myself. It was my wife's and my twenty-fifth wedding anniversary and our family had gathered in a formal dinner to honor us. Jo Ann and I sat there (in the special seats, if you will), in the place of honor while the family members spoke up one at a time, all the way around the table (of almost twenty-five people we care most for). It was an incredibly moving experience and I'll cherish it always, for I know how difficult it was for some of those people to voice their feelings sincerely and in front of everyone. It's a rare moment in our lives when people actually take the time to express some loving thoughts to each other. My wife started crying softly immediately, and I teared up very quickly afterwards. By the time we finished, everyone else had—it was a golden moment I'll always treasure. It occurred to me, later, that this is something of what it's like for those people I intervene upon. I guess you might say I got a taste of my own medicine.

Although the incision is done as gently as possible, it's still a cut, and people often worry that they won't have the right words to convey their love along with the seriousness of their concern. The truth is that once the ice is broken (the intervention specialist's job), the feelings and words tend to flow naturally.

This was particularly evident in a case in which I intervened on a chronic alcoholic who had been addicted to the substance for almost twenty years. We congregated in a hotel room to do the intervention, and the man's employer was one of the twelve participants. The patient was coming under the impression that he would be attending a business meeting. He was well-liked by everyone and he was basically very congenial himself—until the alcohol took over. We walked in and I got the ball rolling with a quiet announcement about why we were all there. I started going around the room for comments; the thoughts were so loving and wonderful, the man shed a lot of tears. One friend told him, "My brother just died in a car accident in a drunk-driving incident—I don't want to have to go to your funeral for the same thing."

Certain topics are what I call "loaded territory," those subjects that are heavy emotional issues for the patient. It seems as if once those areas are entered into, the words and feelings around them just flow for both the participants and the patient. It's such a relief when that barrier of silence is finally broken. For example, some people will mention a deceased family member that they wish were with us now. One woman said to her husband recently, "In three weeks, we'll be celebrating our fortieth wedding anniversary. I want to be with you at the treatment center during family week." The husband broke down and cried. Embracing her, he said, "Okay, let's go."

In another recent case a spouse said to her husband, "For the last three years, whenever you passed out, I watched the video of our wedding and reception. I want us to recapture that moment again." They were both alcoholics, both got help, and today both are outstanding members of a 12-step program.

Once again, as with the case mentioned here, when the person agrees to go into treatment immediately, savor the moment. Let the intervention complete itself—it's a gift that won't get another chance to be given.

EXPLORING & PROBING

The next stage of the "surgery" is to explore the current status of the disease and probe the patient for his feelings about it. This is a matter of timing and chemistry that is learned with experience as an intervention specialist. The participants' words need to be inter-weaved with the suggestion of treatment and an explanation of what treatment entails. The intervention specialist monitors the others' participation based on the needs of the patient.

This exploratory process can be very awkward for everyone and usually involves a fair amount of emotional energy. In a case I did recently in Lake Havasau, the man who was being intervened upon sat holding hands with his wife on one side and his mother on the other the whole time. There was a need for that comfort, but as the intervention specialist I had to see that the women's emotions did not take a turn toward coddling the man as he proceeded through his list of "yeah, buts . . . ." At the same time, I needed to watch to make sure some of the less sympathetic participants didn't convey their impatience with negative gestures. Certain people who hadn't been 100 percent behind the intervention also tended to talk face down (avoiding eye contact), a definite threat to their credibility of being in agreement with treatment for the patient.

The intervention specialist must constantly probe the atmosphere to see how close the patient is to agreeing to treatment. This is a sort of "trial closing" procedure. Some people decide (internally) right away to go to treatment but they are enjoying the attention of the intervention and the plush treatment they're receiving. "Convince me," they challenge the group. It may not be an explicit demand but it's there just the same and it's up to the intervention specialist to determine when the play-acting will be stopped.

On the other side of the coin, when probing the progress of the intervention, it may be clear, early on, that the patient will not go into treatment. My statistics show that those who refuse usually change their minds (anywhere from twenty-four hours to three weeks to six months later). Generally, the intervention specialist needs to prepare himself and the participants for the normal intervention, but must be alert to problems in the procedure and the need for further exploration of the issues. It may be necessary to present an X-ray of the disease—that is, have the participants relay specific examples of the how the addiction is interfering in the patient's (and their) lives. The patient needs to see the urgency of the situation, but, as stated earlier, normally this is not needed.

SUTURE (CLOSING)

With the patient going to treatment, the closing is brief because the patient agrees to treatment, the solution is restated, and encouraging words are given by all present, now that the fear has been diffused. From there, we get up and get the escort team activated. Sometimes, with a volatile patient or a very controlling person, it's better to have the patient agree to seven to ten days of treatment. Examples of his toxic behavior and addictiveness are written down for the therapist at the treatment center, to be brought up in a safe, controlled environment, when the patient is in a less toxic state.

If it appears that the loved one will not acquiesce to treatment, the intervention specialist must see to it that the intervention is ended with dignity and honor—for all parties. There should be no shame in having given the gift even if the person refuses to accept it. No apology for caring. The participants should be prepared beforehand to end with kindness and to support the immediate family. They must be debriefed and made to understand that the fact that the loved one does not go into immediate treatment does not mean that the intervention was a failure. There's no turning back after an intervention—not for the loved one and not for the participants. From that day forward, the silence no longer protects any of them from the reality of the situation; their love has been announced aloud and in front of witnesses, as has the disease and its effects. That puts the responsibility squarely on the shoulders of the patient. It allows the family to solve their problem instead of wallowing in the futile confusion of not knowing what to do for their loved one.

We operate with hope and dignity and suture the wounds gently, but, ultimately, the healing process is the responsibility of the patient, and the rest of the family must get on with their own lives.

FOLLOW-UP

Another phase of intervention surgery is the job of the operating physician (the intervention specialist) to confirm admission with the treatment facility and act as liaison between the new case manager and the family. He should give the case manager assigned to the patient by the treatment facility a verbal report immediately after the patient's admission to the hospital. It's important to make a written report for the therapist and trouble-shoot the case for him/her, outline the potential problem areas, sensitive issues, questionable behavior, etc.

The intervention specialist remains in touch with both the patient (through the case manager or therapist) and the family (through the contact person) to help recognize and overcome delayed reactions by both the patient and the family. An intervention is a very intense ordeal and even when it ends with the person going to treatment (a celebrated event), the participants can suffer from depression or ill health from having been so emotionally drained. Another point to realize is that the entry into treatment is actually just the beginning. There's a lot of work yet to be done, by everyone (patient and family)!

In my practice, I also send out an evaluation form at the end of each intervention to get feedback on my services and to show where I need improvement. These evaluations have been wonderful learning tools and often include glowing testimonials I truly treasure.

When a patient doesn't go in for treatment, the follow-up process actually involves more time. I spend time massaging the family in their disappointment, referring them to other resources for help, untangling any of the details that had been prearranged with a facility.

The final stage of the operation is recovery, and it's up to the patient. Addictive disease is the most treatable untreated disease in the world. Once the patient has been medically led to a point of remission (usually through 100 percent abstention from the addictive substance), he/she has the choice of maintaining abstinence. Recovery is not a matter of eliminating the toxic substance from the person's environment; it's a way of living with the toxic presence without being affected by it. Treatment gets the substance out of the system and stabilizes the disease, but it's up to the patient to maintain that stabilization. Relapse is not a return of the disease, but a collapse of the patient's resolve to be responsible for him/herself. It can and does happen and it can be overcome, but the end result still lies with the patient. In other words, you want to attain physical sobriety as well as psychological sobriety.

True recovery, abstention from addictive substances, comes quickest and easiest when there is a quality recovery of the entire family. The patient and family get involved through therapy and self-help or anonymous groups and thereby change their way of life together, permanently. They approach life one day at a time. Alumni groups, after-care treatment, recovery houses, therapists, etc. are all added support toward recovery, assisting the patient and family with continuous support and getting the disease you have to work *for* you instead of *against* you. The bottom line is you've got to utilize what has been given as your follow-up treatment plan. Otherwise, you're dancing on awfully thin ice.

VIGNETTE—THE SNAKE THAT WENT UP THE DRAIN

It was a crisp, sunny winter morning in upstate New York when Mrs. Wilson stood at the kitchen sink doing her dishes. She watched out the window as the kids played in the alleyway between her old brick apartment building and the one next door. She felt as happy as the kids outdoors to have the sunshine back. Now that her husband was off to work, she was busy with her own chores, deciding to do a load of laundry after she finished the dishes so she could hang them out on the line and really take advantage of the bright day. Well, that's what she planned. What she didn't plan was an uninvited visitor.

He didn't knock, didn't speak, but when the foreign stranger came face to face with Mrs. Wilson through the drain in her sink, she screamed her head off and came within seconds of having a heart attack. One minute her hand was rubbing a sponge across a plate in the warm, sudsy water and the next a gigantic, protruding live snake forced the stopper from her drain and brushed her wrist and the back of her hand as it pushed to the surface for air.

"Ahhhhhhhhhhhhhh!" she yelled, trembling as she tried to dial 911, keeping her eye on the snake that was now slithering over the kitchen cupboard. "It's still coming!" she told the emergency operator. By this time, Mrs. Wilson was on top of a chair trying to figure out where to go next if the police didn't get there in two minutes.

Well, the police did get there right away, and that's what led to my involvement in the case—sort of. After catching the slithering escapee, they started knocking on doors in the apartment building to see if they could find its home. After two floors and twenty-three doors, they were about ready to throw in the towel, except they weren't really equipped to detain the pet (if it was a pet) down at the precinct. One of the officers rapped against the next door and was about to inquire, when a young college man flung the door wide open!

"Herman!" he exclaimed, cupping the face of the snake in his hands, as much as you can cup a snake's face. "Where have you been? I've been looking all over for you!"

"I take it this is your pet," the other officer said, glad

to unwind the creature from his arms. "May we come in?" It was a moot question, for the policeman stepped inside before the question was completed. "What's your name?"

"Billy," the college kid answered, taking the snake over to its empty cage.

"What's all this, Billy?" the cop asked, staring at the drug paraphernalia spread out carelessly over the coffee table. Another rhetorical question.

It was then that Billy was arrested and only a week or two later that he was visited back at his apartment by an old school buddy from the West Coast. Billy was laughing at the whole escapade as he relayed the tale to Jim, but his friend saw the truth.

Billy and Jim had been best pals in school ever since Toby "the Tonka" Power had stolen Jim's dessert in the third grade and Billy had danced his way around the heavyweight bully and got it back for him (even if it had meant getting it all over his shirt). They went through all the Little League sports, California summers at the beach, the girl-chasing and heartaches and proms of high school together. Then, from out of nowhere, Billy was accepted at a prestigious university back east and left. Neither one of them had anticipated how much they would miss each other; they'd been together for so long, they just took it for granted, and sharing by phone just wasn't enough. Jim still had their other friends, their familiar surroundings and old haunts to help him move on, but Billy had really felt isolated these past two terms. In a nutshell, he was lonely, felt out of place, away from friends and family, and he was freezing to boot. He'd never appreciated the California sun as much as he did that winter in New Jersey.

Jim didn't contradict Billy's casual attitude—he went along with him and enjoyed the visit. But the situation nagged at him. He knew what Billy was going through with the drugs and what it would ultimately lead to. He knew for a fact. He knew because he was a recovering addict himself. And that's how Jim knew me and how I got to know Billy.

I was doing a live radio talk show, talking about drug and alcohol addiction, when I got a call from a listener up in San Francisco.

"Ed Storti," the man said, "I don't know if you'll remember, but you did an intervention about two years ago on a young kid in high school in Santa Ana. You saved my life!"

"What's your name?"

"Jim. My parents had called for the intervention—you guys had rousted me up on a Saturday morning a week after I'd wrecked my dad's car in a drag race across a campus parking lot."

"Yes, yes, Jim, I remember very well. How are you doing?" I asked. It's wonderful to hear good news from someone you cared for and were able to help out before.

"Well, I'm doing just fine," Jim went on. "I'm a math major in college, work a little, play a lot, and I enjoy everything, one day at a time. But, Ed—" he said with his voice trailing off.

I was afraid to ask but I had to know: "What is it?"

"Well, I have this friend—Billy," he said, "you might even remember him. He was at my intervention. The tables are turned now, and I think he needs your help."

And that's how I came to know Billy. We talked, and Jim called Billy's mother. He explained what was going on with her son and shared his concern with her. Two days later, Mrs. Templeton called me, and when Billy came home for Easter vacation that spring, it was to begin with an intervention.

Just for the record, it was a very successful intervention. Billy didn't return to the school back east, choosing instead to go in for immediate treatment. Upon completion of his treatment, he transferred to a structured-living/sober-living residence, gaining further insight into himself and his life. Oh, by the way, Herman (the snake) was given to a pet store, where he's allowed a lot of freedom to roam about—except for in the back room where the sink is.

Essential Tidbits

This chapter describes the nuts and bolts of a motivational intervention, the phases of encouragement and respect given to the person with the addiction, and the levels of energy that flow through the process.

FOUR LEVELS OF ENERGY

There are four major areas that keep the energy flowing smoothly through an intervention. These are: a) the mix of people present at the intervention; b) the audio/ visual aspects; c) the positive character traits of the patient that are presented; and d) letters of encouragement. Taken separately, each component has its own energy, and the four types will vary in degree of importance for different people. For instance, I've worked with some families who were so cohesive, loving and enthusiastic as a group, that neither I nor the group needed to say much. The strength and spirit of the group moved the entire intervention to the point that we didn't even read the letters of encouragement of the people who couldn't be present for the intervention, leaving them instead for the patient to take with him to treatment with other letters already written by the group.

In other cases, the people mix has been relatively flat and it has been very important for me to incorporate audio/visual effects such as tape recordings, photos and/or videos, and readings of excerpts from the letters of encouragement to instill the urgency and zeal in the situation. For instance, I once intervened on a twenty-eight-year-old man in Seattle who felt nothing from the presence of the group. He wasn't moved even to respond verbally, much less commit himself to treatment. In short, the intervention was going nowhere, and I was forced to look at some alternatives in the presentation. I brought out a tape from his grandfather, someone who represented some definite "loaded territory" for the young man. His eyes welled up with tears as soon as he heard the old man's voice.

"You know, this is a day I wish I could be there with you, Jimmy, but I'm too ill. But I want you to do this one thing for me. You've got to do this for me."

Immediately, the patient looked up and said, "I'll do it. Let's go."

Sometimes the patient is easily moved emotionally and adds another dimension of energy to the presentation himself that can influence the intervention in a positive or negative manner. But when the atmosphere becomes static, it's good to have a few tools to pull out of the bag (like videos or letters from people the patient has a special fondness for). In the case I just mentioned, the audio/visual connection literally saved the intervention.

The combined impact of the four elements, however, can catapult a person with an addictive disease into immediate treatment. This is the level we always seek; sometimes it evolves naturally out of one or more of the types, while at other times the intervention specialist must manufacture it on the spot with every component available. This is an aspect of interventions that cannot be taught, but must be learned (by the specialist), and an aspect that keeps any guarantees from being promised for the family.

Looking at the people mix, there needs to be variety of voices and personalities, but they must be unified in their intent. That is, they are all present because they want to love the person into treatment. Negative people and negative comments should be strictly limited, if permitted at all. The people mix also refers to ages in the group and relationships to the patient. Sometimes, the closest person (by blood) may carry little power in the patient's opinion, while an outsider (such as a friend, professional peer, or teacher) will make a difference just by being there, without uttering a word.

The audio/visual element, the combination of hearing and seeing different people who mean something special to the patient, involves nonpeople artifacts.

Thirdly, the positive character traits of the patient himself can foster a high level of energy. The group focuses on the positives of the patient, not the negatives. The energy is of excitement and inspiration, not condemnation or confrontation.

Letters, cards, and notes of encouragement by the

intervention participants are usually written before the presentation and passed on to the escort team to give to the patient for use during treatment. These are sources of continued support for the patient's recovery, to remind the patient that he is not alone in his hope and efforts toward recovery. Often, the family does not have physical contact with the patient for the first week or so of treatment, so the cards and letters come in handy as far as being with the person in spirit. The whole batch of letters is given to the patient to provide a continuous stream of supportive consciousness.

TIME COMMITMENT

Another area that affects everyone involved in the intervention and that can bolster the intervention presentation (or wear it down) is the time commitment required of all participants. Staging an intervention is a very involved process. It may happen in a relatively short period (one or two days), but it demands a lot of time and energy on the part of the specialist and the participants, in both the planning stage and the therapeutic work after the presentation. This should not be minimized. The participants must take time to learn about the intervention process, its hopes and risks, discuss the logistics of staging the event, writing down specifics for the intervention specialist and following through after the intervention.

One of the things the intervention specialist stresses during the initial assessment and preparation is that the participants must use this event to mark the start of their own progress, as well as that of the patient. That is, they must commit to seeking help for themselves (immediate family), whether it be through personal counseling, anonymous meetings, reading/writing exercises, whatever. The point is that regardless of what decision the patient makes about treatment, the participants (immediate family) must decide to make certain changes on their own behalf. Such a decision naturally requires quite a time commitment.

MEMO TO THE THERAPIST

One of the jobs of the intervention specialist is to detail the patient's primary addiction and/or problem and his/her particular issues for the treatment therapist. This is a means of both forewarning the therapist and bridging the gap (for the patient) between the intervention and treatment. It provides some measure of consistency with the patient having to explain everything that's taken place up to this point. Of course, points referred to during the intervention (reasons for and descriptive behavior) are barely touched upon even if stated, whereas they are dealt with in depth during treatment. The family is asked to write these memos so the intervention specialist can include them in his final report to the therapist.

The memo also serves to alert the therapist to specific concerns about the patient's behavior and possible "threats" to the admission (such as rage and hostile behavior). Whether the patient sees the memo is up to the therapist; sometimes it is used as evidence of past behavior and to remind the patient about the reality of his situation.

BASIC INCIDENTALS

This area primarily covers the instructions and logistics of conducting an intervention. These are the ABCs of an intervention and for purposes of simplicity, this information is arranged in a question/answer format.

Where is the intervention held?

Virtually anywhere. Since the surprise element is crucial to the intervention process, the intervention site is often the patient's home, early in the morning, just as he's getting up. Otherwise, one of the participants brings the patient to the site (which may be a rented conference room, a friend's home, someone's office, or wherever). The important thing about choosing a site is picking a place you can guarantee the patient will be.

Years ago I intervened in the parked recreation vehicle of one of the participants, a beautiful eight-sleeper, with complete bath and kitchen. We gave our presentation and it went well. The addicted person agreed to go for treatment and as I was closing, the RV-owner popped up and asked if he shouldn't just start the engine and drop off the patient at the treatment center. It was a spontaneous suggestion and none of us got an answer out of our mouths before we were toodling down the 405 Freeway toward San Diego. In that intervention, the whole group was part of the escort team. I don't think it would work if you planned it that way; it just happened to fit in, that day, with that group of people.

If the intervention will be held in a home, put out the pets, take the phone off the hook, turn off the television and radio, show everyone where the bathroom is, and keep refreshments in another room until the presentation is complete. (Hopefully, a gardener will not be operating a leaf-blower at that time.)

Make sure all the participants know where to meet (the rendezvous point) before approaching the patient as a group. Usually, the participants gather together twenty minutes before approaching the patient so they can meet the patient as a group. Make sure everyone knows how to find the pre-meeting place and knows what time to be there. Subsequently, the group caravan over to the intervention site should be slow, with parking available close to the site.

So the intervention site can be anywhere—do you need any particular furnishings or facilities?

It works best to have all the participants sit in a circle with the patient, so adequate seating should be provided. However, I have done interventions in a hallway, standing up. It depends on what is available at the time when the patient is present.

As to the seating arrangement, it is important to be aware of certain views (whether beautiful and inspiring or simply active and interesting). The patient's back should be to the "view" so that he cannot divert his attention there. Likewise, any glare from a window should be anticipated and minimized either by the curtains or by the seating arrangement. The main idea is that you want as few distractions as possible to interfere with the intervention, as it gathers momentum in single-mindedness.

If audio cassettes or videos will be used, make sure the equipment is ready and available to use. Letters and cards (or videos) from people who couldn't be present should be available to the intervention specialist at the preparation meeting and given to the patient at the end of the intervention. The letters have all been written assuming the person accepted the solution presented. Sometimes, flowers (or books or photographs) are also given to the patient to take to treatment.

What time of day is an intervention usually held and how long does it last?

The time and place of the intervention is critical because you want to guarantee the availability of the patient. Early morning (even if you have to wake up the patient to do this) is typically the time of day when a person is least toxic, an advantage for the participants. However, you want to be sure the patient feels (and is) cosmetically together enough to feel comfortable being seen. This seems to be especially true for women, so we usually have a friend call the patient a day prior to the intervention and let her know she (or he) will be coming by for coffee or something. (The least deceit possible is always advised.)

The actual intervention may last from half an hour to two or three hours; it depends on how moved the patient is by the group's presence and how the group dynamics flow. Some people just cut to the quick, say what they have to say, and are done with it. Sometimes patients want to savor the moment by hearing every last word from each participant.

Just recently, I had a patient come out to the living room, see the group of people gathered there, and say, "Okay, I'll go. Let's just go." I got him to sit down, telling him to take just a few moments to at least listen to the love that all those people wanted to give to him.

"Savor the moment," I told him. "Then, we'll go."

Who are the participants?

The participants can be a group of eight or twelve people (more or less). These people are chosen in the planning stage and can often be from out of town and only flying or driving in for the preparation and intervention. They have been briefed (through handouts or by the nucleus of the group) about the process prior to arriving at the preparation meeting site.

Another way to look at the participants is by seeing their roles in the intervention. There are labels I've given to certain people in the group to help ease the intervention through to successful completion. One is "the diffusers." These are the two people who have the most influence with the patient and they are usually the ones who go after the patient if he bolts out of the room, to talk to him privately or basically to calm the patient by their presence. Once in a while, the patient has to be awakened—it's rare, but it does occur (more often with men than with women). The person who would wake up the patient would be someone other than the spouse. The "guardian angel" is the person(s) who acts as a buffer between spouses (if one is also the patient) and the group. This person helps the person pack and stays with the patient at the patient's home or intervention site, just helping to make certain things get done after the intervention. (You see, everyone has role.)

Give me your last-minute rally to the group before we meet the patient.

"W-W-B-D" (We Won't Be Denied!). We have come to present a gift we are proud to give, to someone we love, and we're going to do it. Whether or not he/she accepts it is a separate issue. This is a special time for everyone involved.

How do you start the intervention once you're face to face with the patient?

Walking in to the intervention should be done as a group with chins up, heads high, and positive carriage. Two people with a calming presence should sit on either side of the patient leaving the most powerful person to sit across from him.

The intervention conversation is led by the specialist who monitors and directs the order and duration of the various phases of the process. Private conversations during the intervention between participants are not allowed.

What usually happens at an intervention?

At the actual intervention, the presence of the group diffuses the patient's energy and the person is often quiet, calm. Some cry, some get angry, some bring out their dark humor, some get distant or aloof, and some get aggressive. Only rarely (less than one in a hundred) does the patient become antagonistic and display a volatile reaction to the point that they rant and rave, storm out of the presentation, and can't get past their hostility even to hear out the group. Usually, the addictive drug and age dictate this reaction.

Are we expected to volunteer to speak or do we just go around the circle? Is this real serious talk or can we laugh?

The specialist will call on you individually and direct the conversation based on the chemistry of the people mix. The preparation prior to the intervention will show the strengths and weaknesses of the group. When you are called upon to speak, be yourself first, and "Always Be Caring" (ABCs of the Storti model of intervention). Sympathize, without allowing the patient (and yourself) to see him as the victim of a surprise attack.

Don't pamper the patient; that is, don't coddle him in his insecurity about the whole intervention presentation.

Another important word of advice to the participants is to stay unified. Don't diffuse the power of the group by apologizing for giving this gift of defending your words and actions. There's no need to okay everything with the patient or the other participants; just be sincere and honest. Be yourself. Everyone is there for the same purpose—to inspire the patient to get immediate treatment, and they're all there for the same reason—because they love or respect things about the patient. Breaking character with that common basis will only fragment the group and lessen its effectiveness.

What do we actually say or talk about?

You tell the patient how much he means to your life, something positive in nature about him and how concerned you are, yet that with this solution, you are proud to be in front of him. If you haven't been aware of the addiction or are aware, you still come from a point of love and motivation, saying you're proud to be part of the group and see nothing but positive things coming from this gift to the patient. You point out memories of good times with the patient and tell him how special he is to you. Some groups, if needed, will point out specific instances of the patient's behavior under the control of the addiction and state feelings about the incident, but you don't want to shoot accusatory darts at him with your own anger or grief. You offer the solution—immediate treatment—and assure him that all of the details have been worked out so he can go get help freely.

In the midst of all these things being said, the intervention specialist does some trouble-shooting to identify and dilute the "yeah, buts" the patient will bring up to counteract the idea of going into immediate treatment. The patient must be heard out and the group must be prepared with solutions. These are issues the participants would have brought up (anticipating the patient's concerns) in the initial assessment and preparation and the intervention specialist must pay close attention to them from the beginning. Many times, just by the presence of certain people, the "yeah, buts" are answered. The money issue is a common "yeah, but" that must be diffused by the group. The treatment is to be presented with "red carpet" handling—everything is all set!

One time (and never, ever again) we had to ask a patient for a deposit on the treatment center costs. It was much worse than awkward. Imagine the warmth and sincerity and overall caring that surface during an intervention, the great relief that is felt when the addictive disease has been named aloud and hope has been given through the gift of the treatment solution. All of a sudden, you slip in a little request for money and the whole presentation is cheapened and questionable. Do these people really care about me or are they trying to sell me something? As I said, I did have to ask for money from the patient once, but I will never do it again. It's just not part of the Storti "Honorable Approach to Motivational Intervention."

Does the patient speak or are we all just telling him our feelings?

The patient sometimes responds to things being said about him or to him. However, due to the awkwardness of the moment and the patient's hesitation to speak his feelings aloud, participants often jump in at the slightest pause on the part of the patient. It's important to allow moments of silence for him/her to digest what is being said and not have it glossed over in a rush of words just because the quietness is uncomfortable.

Remember not to engage in side conversations, allowing the patient to fragment the group. The intervention specialist should prevent the patient from holding a "private" conversation with select members of the group or conjuring up a separate deal. Sometimes, the combination of two or more people in the group (including the patient) is intense in a very positive way and then I will allow that conversation more time and latitude.

Why is it necessary to insist on immediate treatment?

The group must be aware that results from the intervention will be both immediate and prolonged. The "now" part of the solution is a result of all of the support being present at that moment, to walk the patient to the treatment center with dignity, with people who care about the patient. Many people don't have these support networks in their lives and have also often intellectualized their disease to a point of denying they need any support. "Now" ensures that professionals are in place at the treatment center too, standing by ready to help move the disease into remission. Whether or not the patient goes into immediate treatment, he/she will never be the same.

There is a risk that the presentation will not be heard out (by the patient) or that it may be misinterpreted as a conspiracy by the group. The patient may not have the same closeness to the group members as he did before the intervention. These risks are there in every group, another reason why the "nowness" is important. Some patients just get stuck on the idea of a three to four week stay. An alternate treatment plan ("Just try it for seven days," for example) may be presented by the intervention specialist, but this is something that should be ironed out in the preparation to ensure the unity of the group. This alternative treatment plan is a means of extending the intervention, which can be very effective in further motivating the patient to go to treatment. Once he's there, in a controlled environment, and has had some individual therapy and time to reflect, he's more likely to stay for the full term.

How does the intervention specialist stress the importance of immediate treatment?

Usually a closing statement is presented by the intervention specialist, such as "Make a commitment to accept the solution and go all the way with it—stay for full treatment." This statement works as an indicator of how much more energy will be needed or required from the group. In the actual intervention the specialist has a couple of other specific techniques to use in working toward the common goal. One is referred to as "C-B-A," Close By Assuming (that the patient is going to treatment). There is documented success in the idea of preconceived belief in the expectation of acceptance. Trial closing (looking to close the session with an agreement that the patient will go for treatment) during the intervention is important in keeping tabs on the probability of success, as well as the timing involved with acceptance and the closing of an intervention. If the patient is in physical distress and has agreed, there is no need to continue when you feel it's being overstated. (There is a point at which an overdose can occur with this procedure, which is something the specialist must be aware of at all times.)

There is a window of opportunity with this disease and, many times, the intellect stops the patient from getting help. The intervention is a statement of defying the odds and destiny of the patient and seizing the moment of opportunity!

The patient agrees to go for immediate treatment, then what?

Two or three participants will help the patient pack and will escort him/her to the treatment facility, which has been chosen beforehand by the primary participants. Registration, financial matters, and other administrative-type details will have been worked out a few days before. While the patient is packing, I like to call the treatment facility and tell them the estimated time of arrival so they can make any necessary preparations. Incidentally, although it's common for the spouse to accompany a patient to a hospital (negotiable), he should not do it alone. There should always be a person who has significant "presence" to serve as a buffer for the patient.

Is this a happy occasion?

It is difficult occasion for ultimate happiness. It is a very sensitive time for everyone and usually lots of tears flow. But when a patient agrees to treatment, it is also a time of rebirth—an occasion to celebrate. No balloons and cake but lots of love and hugs.

Sometimes, the group wants to have a photograph taken after the intervention presentation to mark the occasion. (If anticipated, the camera and film should be readily available.) Others don't feel this and in fact, a "funeral air" prevails over the group.

What happens after the escorts leave to take the patient to the treatment center?

At the end of an intervention, there is some debriefing. Being of a high level of energy, an intervention is an emotionally draining experience; everyone needs a few minutes afterwards to relax and unwind. I always try to emphasize savoring the moment and discuss possible delayed reactions.

Debriefing is especially important when the patient chooses not to go in for immediate treatment. The group needs to be massaged back into focusing on the fact that they did what they could—it's really up to the patient to use the gift or not. When the patient does go to treatment, I usually follow up with phone calls to both the treatment end and the family side of the case until I'm assured everything is going smoothly. It's also important to warn the family to be somewhat on guard for the first seventy-two hours a patient is in treatment. This is when he/she is most susceptible to his fears and wants to beg someone to "get me out of here!"

The family should leave their letters of encouragement with the escort group and then stay away from the patient for about five days, checking on the status of the situation only through the therapist.

The group members must take care of themselves. There is a very real powerlessness for the group in the results of time after the intervention. All they can do (for the patient) is present the solution—then, it's up to him/her.

After the debriefing and after the patient has been left at the treatment center, then what? Is there a delayed reaction for the patient or the participants?

Everyone will have a delayed reaction—it only varies in degree as to intensity. No one is ever the same after an intervention; the silence is broken, the secret is out. The solution has been presented. There's no turning back.

The delayed reaction for the patient who goes for treatment can be met with the cards and letters of encouragement and can surface and be diffused in therapy. If the patient's reaction is one of bitterness, anger, outrage, euphoria, whatever—the treatment facility has qualified people on hand to help them cope with it.

For the patient who didn't go to treatment, a delayed reaction may be that he/she goes at a later time, on his/her own.

For the group members, however, they have to work their own contingency plan, using a therapist, anonymous groups, and staying detached with love. They have begun to de-emphasize the importance of the patient and they can turn to each other for help. They may have to deal with delayed reactions in the form of depression, disappointment, and the effects of being exhausted (emotionally), etc. Yet, some will encounter the win/win philosophy that they need to try, and can accept whatever results.

What about six months or two years down the road—
what if the patient goes back to using (the drug of
choice)?

Relapse is always a possibility. Basically, there are four steps to alter relapse:

a) fracturing the code of silence (a group intervention is very forthright and powerful for pointing out the disease). Some patients have stated that when they thought about using alcohol/drugs they thought about the group and it brought them back to reality.

b) involving the family in the patient's treatment and learning about the co-dependency and how the family gets addicted to the loved one. They must participate to break the chain of being enablers and the chain of control.

c) getting patient and family aftercare, whether it be individual and/or family counseling, anonymous groups, etc. They must continue in a plan of action or their mindset will drive them back to addiction and co-dependency.

d) allowing time for the results to take place. Some folks want quality results in three days. The intervention is only a start; the first year is the most sensitive, more is revealed as you go on.

Despite the potential for relapse, an intervention is generally a one-time-only effort. A second intervention later on would be counterproductive and only serve to enable the patient's addiction!

What kinds of things could go wrong in an intervention?

Many things can go wrong but not many do. There are certain behavior patterns, opinions, and attitudes I refer to as red flags, because they alert me to possibly explosive issues in the assessment. For example, in the assessment people may indicate that the patient displays bizarre behavior (walks around threatening people or plays with guns, etc.), or that the patient is ultra-fragile (in health or spirit). The intervention specialist must pay close attention to what is being said, because the family members (being somewhat accustomed to the behavior) frequently understate the reality or downplay its significance, without realizing it. The following is a list of items I consider to be red flags—things I consider very seriously before recommending an intervention be held at all:

- when the spouse or severe co-dependent has less than one year of his/her own recovery efforts

(in other words, they have been treated for their pathology and are still on shaky ground)
- when the patient is very theatrical and has a history of upstaging events
- when the patient is highly aggressive
- when the patient has tried suicide before
- when the patient is prone to filing lawsuits
- when the patient has a history of being violent and abusive
- when the patient abuses the spouse
- when there are weapons in the home
- when there is unrest in the nucleus of the group
- when the patient is known to be unapproachable
- when there is a lack of documentation of the problem/no primary diagnosis
- when the patient threatens to withdraw his love
- when the patient is highly pampered (common among young adults; the family gives mixed messages to the person)
- when the patient has an overwhelming sense of self-destructiveness
- when the patient is known to exhibit severe defiance
- when the patient has a history of bolting out of the room.

All red flags indicate the need for another plan or a softer approach and more profound assertions on the part of the group and the intervention specialist. They may also point to other alternatives (besides intervention) and tough-love ways of handling the situation (such as cutting off financial support). All red flags are present in each case; they vary as to extent and intensity, but they are negotiable, workable, and must be assessed.

What would cause an intervention to erupt?

As a close parallel to red flags, there are several main things that can cause an intervention to erupt. One is a poor assessment. The initial conference an intervention specialist has with the contact person must be detailed and long enough to allow the specialist to explore the red flag areas. One problem specialists may have with this is that they don't have enough experience with performing interventions to ask the right questions to find out the important information. Another point to consider is that the intervention procedure itself is not foolproof; it's not for everyone. The therapist or specialist has to consider this fact from the very beginning. There are some families who are so desperate they will not take no for an answer, yet, as a specialist, you must be honest and ethical.

A second reason for eruption lies in a poor preparation by the specialist. He shouldn't be rushed by the family's impatience to "get it over with." The details of the process, as well as the patient's condition, must be carefully outlined and discussed. Another thing that signifies a poor preparation is not addressing the "yeah, buts."

When there's no chemistry in the group (which is no one's fault), it can sabotage an intervention. The power of the group's presence is one thing, but the power of that combination of people can have an even greater impact. If the intervention ends prematurely, the intervention can end in an eruption. This is an issue of timing the intervention specialist can learn only by experience. He must have a sense of how far to go with the intervention.

The spouse can also threaten the intervention—by backing out of his commitment to the process and/or by turning aggressive during the intervention. In one case I intervened on recently, we got the male alcoholic to enter a treatment center, but he left within twenty-four hours, and his wife, who had pledged to begin her own counseling and setting boundaries, dropped her commitment. She welcomed her husband home with open arms and started sweeping everything under the rug. This action reinforces both his dependency on alcohol and her co-dependency, and puts the children in a true victim mode.

This very disappointing outcome normally doesn't happen for the intervention specialist. Usually, you can gauge the commitment of the spouse and the other participants during the assessment of the whole scenario.

Finally, there are a certain breed of people who are so emotionally detached, they simply cannot be reached. They are incapable of accepting help. Forcing an intervention on such a person could lead to an eruption very quickly.

What are the risks you referred to earlier in this chapter?

There are many risks to holding an intervention. To deny this importance, or worse yet, ignore them (in the assessment), is a dangerous practice for the intervention specialist. Personally, I prefer to go over the risks very clearly and quietly with the family (nucleus group). Some of them I've identified over the years are:

- Timing (for the group and the patient)—is there a need to do this intervention now? If the patient is on a health kick, it might be good to delay intervention. Likewise, if there has been a family tragedy and the family needs time to stabilize or get some other related therapy. You don't want to set up an intervention when it will be competing for preparation time with a wedding or other big family event; there's too much emotion and stress that will accompany the intervention by itself.
- Disappointment when the patient won't go to treatment; can they handle this result if it occurs that day.
- Patient bolting out of the room (young women on crystal meth and men in their thirties addicted to cocaine can be prone to this).
- The outcome of the treatment: you can get well or you can be dishonest and think you can have the drug "one more time." The process itself is a risk. Ultimately, it is the patient's own responsibility.
- Distortion—the patient misreads the intent of the intervention.
- Vindictiveness—the patient creates a cold war with the group members and/or plays one person against the other.
- Change—the commitment of the immediate family to lessen the emotional strain for themselves,

get help for themselves, and stop the roller-coaster ride through continuous crisis situations.

- Suicide after an intervention is a possibility. I am not aware of a suicide that resulted from the intervention process, but I also like to point out that being active in addictive disease is suicidal in itself.
- Confidentiality—there's a risk in telling people about the intervention (even to solicit their participation) because they may tip off the patient. The family must decide who needs to know and who should not know.
- An ununified group—regardless of what the patient does, the group can't go backwards; they must be unified in believing that the intervention was the right thing to do.

These are all risks that should be admitted to and considered by both the intervention specialist and the people participating in the intervention. You may not be able to eliminate them, but you can minimize the probability of their happening beyond what you can handle and make plans about how you will compensate in the event that they do occur.

VIGNETTE—MARINATED IN MALIBU

It hadn't rained (significantly) in Southern California for over five years, but I was watching the huge, elongated waterdrops lashing the trees outside my office window on the fourth day of torrential downpours when I got a desperate call from Linda. I could tell from her voice she had made the call several times without actually dialing the phone, before she finally connected with me. Then, it turned out to be a "mobile" call—that is, she wanted me to come to her in Pacific Palisades.

"It's just that my husband's a producer and I'm a model; our schedules are so tight that we can't coordinate driving out to San Gabriel Valley to see you," she explained.

Reluctantly, I agreed, but I had no idea what I was in for. The drive to the coast is an hour and a half on a sunny day, if it's not between 6 A.M. and 9 A.M. or between 2 P.M. and 7 P.M., and here I was, starting out from Pasadena at three o'clock in the afternoon. The rain kindly took a moment's break while I gassed up and found my way to the Santa Monica freeway. After that, it was a pretty smooth drive, considering visibility was about one and a half car lengths; the rain was slicking up the highway and causing accidents all over the place. It's a standard joke in sunny California that the drivers don't know how to drive in any weather but clear (clear smog, that is). Anyway, I managed to stay on the road and out of the fender-benders and finally got off the highway in Pacific Palisades at a quarter after six. It had been a long time since I'd driven up Pacific Coast Highway, but today was not the day to be there.

The ocean waves jumped up to splash the rain and play tag in a frenzy they seldom get to enjoy. All I could think about was how inadequate the retaining walls looked. But I should have been watching the road instead of the sea, anyway. A mudslide had caught someone's attention ahead and—wham! they went into the side of an oncoming car, blocking the whole road. My appointment with Linda was scheduled for seven, which would have been fine, but for the accident. I sat there unable to turn off the highway and into the hills to find their house.

"What a relief to finally arrive," I confessed and gratefully accepted a cup of decaf. The house was huge and gorgeous, perched on a bluff with only three others overlooking the ocean. Linda and Frank (her husband) led me into the living room, which was plush and elegantly simple as far as decor went.

"It's my sister, Josie," she told me. "She's an alcoholic and injects crystal meth. She lives with three guys who are all drug addicts; I know she's slept with all of them—I'm afraid she'll get AIDS on top of everything else. She's only thirty-two. I want to do an intervention on her. She was arrested two weeks ago and her court date is in two more weeks, but if we don't do something now, I don't think she'll live that long!"

"That's a big agenda of heavy problems, Linda," I told her. "Have you thought about going through the legal system?"

"What do you mean?"

"I mean reporting the situation to the court, having them assign her to a treatment center and—"

"Oh, no! I couldn't!"

She didn't let me finish. In complicated cases like this in which the person cannot be rational at all, it often works to let the judge remand the chemical dependent to a treatment facility as an alternative to jail. Linda was crying in her husband's gentle embrace and I wasn't sure what to say.

A week later, I met with eight other people for the intervention on Josie. Her father was deceased, but her mother came, and Josie's Uncle Jim, Linda and Frank, and four miscellaneous Hollywood friends came. Everyone had known Josie for a long time and came out of the fondness they had for the person she used to be. It seemed they were all afraid she would kill herself (accidentally) at any moment. The love in the group was genuine and substantial; it was the first time I felt halfway good about the case.

I hadn't ignored the red flags, and I warned Linda and the others from the start that this was precisely the type person who usually bolted from the premises before the presentation could be made—that is, if they could meet with her in the first place. I feared a no-show from the very beginning.

Two of the friends made arrangements to pick up Josie a couple of corners from the house where she lived. I presumed it was by mutual consensus that no one visited Josie at her home. I felt uneasy about the arrangement; it seemed so iffy to me. Late in the evening on the night before the intervention was to take place, I got a phone call from one of the friends in the group named Bob.

"One of the boyfriends she lives with was murdered," he told me.

"What happened?"

"He was driving her car and pulled into the alley behind a liquor store and someone put a gun to his head. Word got back to the house that he was killed because he owed some money to certain people."

"Where's Josie now?"

"At home, I guess. I don't know for sure." We hung up and I called Linda to discuss it.

"I think we better cancel this thing," I said, figuring

Josie would be too preoccupied (if she could be found at all) for the intervention to have a beneficial impact.

"We can't cancel, Ed," Linda pleaded with me. "Don't you see? The same thing could happen to her. She's living in danger."

We met at Linda's house early the next morning—gazing out the picture window in the front room of the house, it occurred to me how the tranquility of the sea (the weather was back to normal by this time) contrasted with the turmoil in my heart and stomach. No one could dispute the dire need for some kind of intervention in this case, but I felt more than a little out of my league. I think I was hoping for "divine" intervention.

After waiting for more than half an hour beyond the appointed time, we got a phone call. Josie wasn't at the corner. The energy in the group changed from bad to worse, but the group waited. I suggested they think about writing letters or making a video to be given by an assigned group member if it turned out to be a no-show. Then, we got a second call in which the friend said he found Josie, but was stalling at a fast food spot to check in with the group. By now, two hours had passed since our appointment.

The group was still intact, but the atmosphere was negative and wearisome. I suggested we cancel it and got immediate resistance. They said they were already there, better late than never. I decided that if they were willing, so was I.

At a quarter to two in the afternoon, Josie stumbled in the front door, tear-stained and drained. Even with her hair uncombed and in tattered clothes, she was pretty. Her frenzy was partially drug-induced, partially the remnants of a hangover and partially raw nerves.

I barely introduced myself when she stared at me and shouted, "Get out of my face!" Then, she went on a rampage about last night's events and all the emotions she was going through. I started feeling protective of the group; they had been through a lot trying to coordinate this for her and they didn't deserve to be ignored and abused. I presented treatment and Josie rolled her eyes, crossed her arms over her chest, and slumped down on the floor next to Linda on the sofa. "Forget it!"

I was practically at a loss; her drug-induced defiance was too great (a red flag I had warned them about). Uncle Jim talked to her for a minute or two, and one of her friends was able to help her mellow out a little bit. Suddenly, the whole atmosphere changed. I resumed my role and we went on with almost no resistance. In the end, Linda had said how afraid they all were that she would end up like her boyfriend who had died last night, and Josie looked around the room at everyone. The defiant malice in her eyes had disappeared as she saw the love staring back at her.

"Okay," she said.

I wasn't sure what "okay" meant, so I further explained treatment to her. She stared at me and said, "I need help. I'm a basket case. Whatever or whenever—let's go."

As I followed in the car with her brother driving her to treatment, I realized a divine intervention *had* occurred. Today Josie works in the treatment field of addictive disease as a counselor, and last year she ran in the Los Angeles Marathon.

Getting Started

To intervene is to interrupt, and in our usage here I refer to interrupting a negative pattern of behavior (addiction) in hopes of persuading the patient to take positive action toward redirecting his life. The primary call for intervention help is for a person suffering from a chemical dependency (drugs or alcohol), but compulsive behavior of nearly any kind can be cause for intervention.

There are two types of intervention specialists: the first is the traditional professional who acts in a clinical setting. (The clinical model is more educational in nature, and the group takes more responsibility during the presentation and shares its consequences. It is basically script-oriented, in that participants will read from their prepared written statements.) In the nontraditional type, the intervention specialist is more involved and the presentation is more accelerated, more spontaneous and less academic, resulting in a higher motivational effect. The nontraditional interventionist generally has his or her own office, functions independently, and will usually travel out of state, or wherever, to intervene.

Traditional interventionists are usually on staff at hospitals, treatment centers, or organizations such as the National Council on Alcoholism, and usually stay within their setting or geographic area. In addition to serving as interventionists in these clinical settings, they also often act as public outreach coordinators and/or addictive-disease counselors. Most are highly trained, competent individuals.

There are also capable counselors without the title in high schools who act as interventionists with teenagers.

Marriage and family therapists maintain lots of qualified interventionists and, when asked, will make referrals. Many family therapists do interventions themselves, interweaving their personalities and meshing both techniques.

A small but growing number of interventionists are going the nontraditional route and function independently. There is also a new group called the National Association of Intervention Specialists that has been established to further the goals of the independents. Some individual intervention specialists are willing to intervene in nonclinical settings and truly personalize their services to your needs.

To reach an interventionist, call a reputable hospital or treatment center. Several are listed at the end of the book. Or contact a specific organization such as the National Council on Alcoholism.

The best referral will be from someone who has actually participated in an intervention and has come away with positive feelings about its outcome. Always remember that you are the one who chooses the intervention specialist, so you might talk to a few! I'm amazed at how often I'm called and requested to "do the intervention now," prior to an assessment of the situation, prior to ever meeting the person. They just seem to want to "get the job done" and don't really care who does it. This manner of hiring an intervention specialist is not in the best interests of the family. You want to find someone you feel comfortable with personally, as well as someone who has the credentials you respect. This is even more important with an intervention specialist than it is with a doctor because the intervention specialist and philosophy must be coordinated with you and tailored to your situation. It's not a simple matter of applying his exclusive professional expertise to one person.

QUALIFICATIONS

Currently, there are no specific licensing requirements or certification programs for interventionists. Some interventionists hold undergraduate and/or graduate degrees in psychology or sociology. Some are certified alcoholism/drug counselors or marriage and family therapists.

Many professionals decide to become intervention specialists after their own recovery from addiction to alcohol or some other substance, such as cocaine, heroin, food, etc. Their experience had led them to a new plane of compassion and now they want to actively help others. But do not choose an interventionist solely on the basis of whether or not he or she is in recovery from an addiction. Feeling confident and comfortable with the person you choose to represent you is by far the most important factor.

To explore an interventionist's methods, qualifications, and success, it's appropriate to ask for names and phone numbers of former clients and contact some of these people. Other referral sources are people who have participated in interventions—relatives, colleagues, and friends of clients.

Selecting an interventionist is much like choosing your physician or attorney. People seeking professional help will usually find an appropriate way to assess that person's qualifications before initiating contact. Ask around for referrals and follow-up by talking with a few. Be objective and be honest with yourself. Then go with the one you're most comfortable with; trust your instincts.

TRACK RECORD OF THE INTERVENTIONIST

When talking about a "track record," you want to be clear as to what is being tracked. That is, are you asking, "How many years have you been an interventionist?" "How many years have you been in the chemical dependency/counseling profession?" "How long have you been in recovery (if applicable)?" "How many interventions do you hold in a month or a year and what percentage of these result in the dependent person agreeing to go for treatment?" "How many stay for full treatment?" "Do you follow up with the family and the treatment center after the intervention?"

All of these questions imply certain assumptions, and you must remember to take the answers to the questions into consideration with all the other facts. That is, you're primarily trying to gauge the credibility, the commitment and the reliability of the specialist. To date, there is no central organization or agency that keeps detailed records and follow-up statistics on intervention cases, so to a large degree, the answers you get may be self-serving. You can, however, check with the Better Business Bureau for feedback on independent specialists. On the other hand, a long period of time in the business supports the assumption of some degree of success and effectiveness. Otherwise, the interventionist would not be able to maintain his position and support himself or work for a credible organization.

The nature of the interventionist's job is not one that would invite uncaring people into the profession. Most interventionists have a personal goal (as well as a professional one) to get the dependent person into a treatment facility; they're genuinely concerned with the gravity of the disease and are dedicated to doing all they can to stop its progression. A track record and experience in solving unexpected problems are certainly important, but enthusiasm, courage, the desire to help, and willingness to learn can and will carry beginners through many difficult situations.

FEES

Hospitals and treatment centers will sometimes arrange for interventionists on their staffs to do clinical interventions for patients who are going to enter treatment. They consider the intervention part of the cost of treatment. However, an increasing number of facilities are beginning to charge by the hour for the time their staff interventionists devote to interventions.

Independent interventionists charge fees for service much like a personal or family therapist. Their service includes assessing the need to intervene and helping the family find the most appropriate treatment center for the addicted person, as well as appropriate after-care. As in any other profession, the more experienced an individual is and the broader his referral base, the higher his fee. Some charge on an hourly basis, ranging from $100 to $250 per hour. Others charge a fee for the entire process (all-inclusive fees), which range from $250, up to and over $5,000. And some operate on a sliding scale based on the person's ability to pay. Hospital-based interventionists are more flexible (regarding fees) than private specialists, because the hospital can sometimes underwrite the procedure, whereas each intervention (in part or whole) is the bread and butter for the individual specialist.

QUALITIES IN THE INTERVENTIONIST

When I'm lecturing on motivational intervention, people frequently ask, "What qualities would you look for if you were choosing an interventionist to perform an intervention on a member of your family?" So I've tried to isolate the qualities I feel are crucial. I know all the ones I list below aren't going to be achievable by a single human being, and I'm not sure how my clients would rate me by these criteria, but these are qualities I think are especially important. Also, some may not be easily observed, but people seeking an interventionist can try to confirm them through referral sources.

Self-Esteem: Addicted people will sometimes vent their terror and pain on the interventionist because he or she is the person advocating action and change—two things addicted people (and often their families as well) fear and resist. Therefore, the interventionist must be able to remain unaffected by negative energy and know how to turn the group into positive energy. The specialist must be energized and show enthusiasm; he or she has to be able to lead the group through the sensitive issues. Previous clients and intervention participants can often attest whether or not an interventionist has this ability.

Emotional Intuitiveness: This quality should be discernible in the first contact made with an interventionist. He must be gentle and compassionate, yet able to balance those qualities with firm direction when necessary.

The normal screening of emotions often vanishes during addiction crises, so the interventionist will become a temporarily intimate member of a family group and it should be apparent that he views that position as both a challenge, a privilege, and an honor.

Interventionists must know how to allow individuals being intervened upon to retain their dignity, even if they refuse to enter treatment. This is ensured primarily by projecting courtesy, empathy, and a sense of dignity from within themselves.

Professionalism: The interventionist should be professional in dress, grooming, speech, and mannerisms. The physical environment of the setting in which the client is received should be appropriate and reassuring.

Any interventionist who is in recovery must represent the most positive aspects of recovery—physically, psychologically, and spiritually. Hopefully, the intervention specialist will not only do a terrific job during the presentation, but will follow through in all phases of service, including follow-up calls trouble-shooting the cases when necessary.

Motivational Skills: Confidence and credibility can be communicated on the phone through tone of voice and information given, and in person through a facial expression or the quality of a handshake. (There are people who convey that they mean business merely on their handshake.) It is through his motivational skills that the interventionist can convince even resistant participants to take part in an intervention by intuiting where the fine line is between persuasion and alienation, when to step forward and when to step back.

Observing the interventionist accomplish this in the assessment and preparation sessions prior to the actual intervention should go a long way toward confirming his motivational abilities.

Flexibility: As the intervention process unfolds, it should become apparent to family members that the interventionist has the flexibility to switch from motivator to clinician to technician to "Chamber of Commerce member" describing the immediate area. Also, because of the crisis nature of the addictive-disease environment, the interventionist's personality must be flexible enough to accommodate sudden changes in the plans.

Objectivity: Family members experience growing confidence in the interventionist's ability to determine which participants to call on at crucial moments during an intervention and trust in his decisions (mainly used within the nontraditional model).

Commitment: The family should sense the interventionist's compassionate and sincere commitment to working with people in crisis. That compassion is what enables the interventionist to hear and respond to people in pain, prevent catastrophe, and render help.

QUESTIONS TO ASK THE INTERVENTIONIST

Can you admit to a treatment facility other than the one where you are on staff?

Some intervention specialists, like myself, do have the flexibility to admit to a variety of treatment facilities throughout the U.S.

Will you provide names and phone numbers of clients you have worked with in recent months, or your last case?

Any competent interventionist should be willing and able to do this (most families are excited about sharing their experience). Obviously, names would only be given out with prior approval from the clients.

Do you counsel the patient after the patient is in treatment?

Although interventionists monitor patient progress, most "release" the patient to the treatment center therapists so that they are emotionally free to move on to the next intervention. Some specialists can follow a case through treatment and offer aftercare counseling and therapy.

Will you intervene more than once if a patient doesn't go into treatment?

Once a comprehensive intervention has been completed, there is no point in duplicating it. A consultation might be appropriate, but not a full intervention.

Are you yourself recovering from an addictive disease?

Be cautious about an interventionist who can only talk about his own disease and whose knowledge seems limited to that.

If the patient physically bolts or gets verbally excitable, what will you do?

An interventionist should be able to tell you how far he will normally go in this process, what's feasible from his point of view and what's not.

Do you take a hard or soft approach?

It's advantageous to have an intervention specialist who can adapt to whatever is needed in a given situation (hopefully, by combining science and an artistic ability, a loving process).

If certain family members or friends are reluctant to participate in an intervention, what can be done?"

An interventionist should be able to guide you in ways to ask family members, friends, and colleagues to attend a preparation meeting, at which point they can make a decision about whether or not to attend an intervention. On the other side, not every group has the chemistry to go through this process; that's what the assessment is for—to determine if the group can rally together and create a people presence that will have a powerful impact on the patient. Sometimes another assessment is necessary to further unite the nucleus.

What usually happens when you enter an addicted person's home and begin to intervene?

Interventionists should be able to give you both norms and extremes of what they have experienced. What usually happens is that the patient is stunned and sits and listens, the first goal of the intervention.

Do you assist in the admission process at the treatment center?

The interventionist should help accomplish a smooth transition from the intervention close into the admission process. Most interventionists will verbally walk patients and family members through the admission process. The escort team is primed at the preparation meeting.

What can a family member do at the home site to ensure an intervention will go smoothly?

Most interventionists instruct you in detail what to do. Examples: take the phone off the hook; be certain infants are in another room with someone present to see to their needs; put dogs, cats, and other domestic pets outside or in a closed room. All particulars are talked out in the assessment and the preparation and intermittent phone calls prior to the intervention.

Will you abort a scheduled intervention?

The process can be aborted at different stages, at any given time. Some cases have been rescheduled due to circumstances, but once you walk in or the patient walks in—you're on. You must go forward from there. The presentation is in process at that moment, prepared or not. That's my rule of thumb. Also, there are people who are so toxic, so addicted, that a "good time to intervene" simply cannot be planned. You must at least try; sometimes, the intervention will sober them up (so to speak) quite quickly!

Are participants who have addictive diseases themselves allowed to participate?

If an addicted participant that you're considering cannot be trusted because he might warn the person being intervened on about the intervention, most interventionists would strongly suggest you not invite them. The final criterion is the degree of trust the family feels toward a given participant.

Can young children participate in an intervention?

They can, but most interventionists will request an opportunity to assess whether their participation is appropriate. Letters written by children/video or audio tapes are often effective substitutes for their actual participation.

*If a key participant can't attend the preparation
meeting, can that person participate in the
intervention?*

Yes, if an interventionist is willing to prepare the participant by phone and agrees to the participation, or
prepares the participant just prior to walking in.

*Can two family members be intervened with on the
same day?*

Some interventionists have a method to orchestrate
this. Usually an interventionist will intervene with one
in the morning and the other in the afternoon. Based
on age and drug, both can be done at the same time;
it's all possible with the right group, yet, this particular
case always needs a major assessment, the right group
chemistry, and a realization of the type of patients you
can do this with.

*Do you have to have a bottom-line consequence (such
as job termination, separation, or divorce) to ensure
the success of an intervention?*

Some interventionists feel this is necessary, but most
interventions never reach the "or else" stage. Personally, the primary goal in my interventions is to present
the addicted person with a solution to the problem, and
to give the families and friends the peace that comes
from having acted positively and knowing they have
done their best.

*Why aren't outpatient programs as effective as
inpatient programs?*

Within the cocoon-like, sheltered environment of a
treatment center, the addicted are taught to face themselves, their disease, and their frustrations with life as
they are weaned from the mood-altering chemicals
and/or aberrant behavior they have used to relieve or
mask pain. The ideal treatment center staff is made up
of skilled, helping professionals from different disci-
plines who interact purposefully to motivate patients
toward recovery.

Emotional bonding between patients and other people involved in the treatment process is widely acknowl-
edged to be a primary activator of recovery. There is a
much greater opportunity for such bonding to occur
among people who live together twenty-four hours a
day for three or four weeks than there is among people
who see each other two to three hours in the evening,
following days filled with normal work and family activities. Outpatient programs need the patient who is motivated to attend and put their abstinence and attendance as first priority over all outside issues. Outpatient
programs are for the patient who will adhere to total
abstinence and random urine screening for drug use.
Sometimes the inpatient program motivates the patient
to the outpatient level of thinking!

What about short-term inpatient stays?

Short-term programs may be appropriate for people
who are already sincerely motivated to begin recovery
and people who have relapsed and require an intensive
short-term course of recovery treatment. Also, they are

certainly better than nothing for people who can't afford a long-term program or whose insurance coverage will pay only for a short-term program. And when followed by an intensive aftercare program fostering connection to one of the anonymous self-help groups, a short-term program can be very effective.

Speaking of self-help groups, since treatment centers strongly stress leading patients into anonymous self-help groups, why shouldn't patients simply start out there?

Few people I have intervened with were capable of making the strong commitment to the activities required by the 12 Steps of the anonymous groups without first having been exposed to the psychological educational preparation that takes place in a treatment center. The 12 Steps required by the anonymous groups are designed to change the person's lifestyle and behavior through changing his or her actions. Many addicted people don't attend self-help group meetings long enough to acquire the habit of performing the actions that result in behavioral change. After completing an inpatient program (which usually entails working through the first three steps of the self-help group philosophy), however, the patient will have acquired habits of action that enable him to work through the remaining steps to recovery successfully.

How is the family involved with the treatment facility?

A family counseling coordinator conducts an orientation for the patient's family and informs them when family counseling will begin. There are many programs in which the family is included for one week of counseling and the loved one is included at different times within that week. Other programs include the family immediately for small doses of counseling and include the patient at different time.

How are the programs at treatment centers financed?

Health insurance rules and regulations change frequently, but basically, there is no blanket coverage for alcohol/chemical dependency treatment. Some insurance companies contract with certain medical treatment centers, as do some employers, in which cases there may be coverage for the expense. However, there is also a tremendous number of disputes in which a patient has been assured 100 percent coverage by the insurance company, only to have it denied a couple of days into treatment. Consequently, the majority of patients are on a cash basis with the treatment centers. An intake counselor (or business representative) at the treatment center can outline their program costs—whether Medicare or your insurance covers it—and provide a payment schedule for prospective clients.

Are there any independent agencies that monitor treatment centers and provide unbiased reports about how well they provide services?

The Joint Commission Accreditation of Hospitals (which monitors all hospitals) is a major monitoring agency, and many insurance companies demand this accreditation. Bear in mind, though, the "product" of the treatment center is treatment, and if a treatment center is doing its job, that will be affirmed through referrals from patients and its verifiable reputation, its long-standing operation.

Vignette—"I Just Don't Care Anymore"

"Just take a minute to calm yourself," I told the sobbing woman on the phone. "I'll wait here for you." We'd been on the line for almost five minutes but all that I'd gotten out of her, so far, was that she was a med student in her mid-twenties and she was worried about her mother. I listened to her catch her breath and heave a sigh of forced bravery to continue confiding in me, and the sanctity of my role became apparent. I felt truly humbled as I realized I was but one small part of the lifeline that would (eventually) connect the woman's loved one with her own life again.

"She hasn't been outside of the house in months," Jill told me when she felt able to resume speaking.

"What exactly is your mother's problem?" I asked.

"It's her weight. Her name is Doreen and she's fifty-four years old, a diabetic, and she weighs more than 450 pounds. Her knees are so bad she's confined to a wheelchair. She's supposed to have surgery on her knees, but she won't go."

I listened carefully, and having to deal with my own eating compulsions (albeit on a much less extreme basis), I could sympathize easily. This wasn't the first time I had been called to intervene on someone with an eating disorder; the addiction to food has been growing into a serious psychological and medical problem at an alarming rate over the past twenty years, and the victims are getting younger and younger.

"She never eats much around us, just picks at dinner when we're together, but she's alone most of the time and has food brought in—fast food, groceries—by neighbors, kids, anyone who won't be staying to watch her eat it. But all the wrappers are in the trash; we know she eats!" Jill explained. I knew it was very common for people with eating disorders to eat by themselves, to hide food, and to even try to destroy the evidence (wrappers, etc.) as well.

"She's a prisoner in the house because she can't walk! She's just letting her entire life pass by. Last week, she even missed Renee's (Jill's sister) graduation. We shared it with her on video since my brother recorded it, but it wasn't the same—" Jill broke off, succumbing to a few more tears. "We love our mother, Mr. Storti, we want to share our lives with her—not just show them to her on the TV. We want her to be a part of the living with us."

I reassured Jill that I was aware of both the habits and the gravity of the situation of an overeater like her mother. I reminded her that there is hope and that she had just opened the door to it.

Three days later, I left my home when it was sunny in San Pedro, but not nearly as hot as it was out in Rancho Mirage, California, where I drove to Jill's house for the intervention. We had done a conference call preparation with Robie (Doreen's husband), the other siblings in the family, and all four parents of Doreen and Robie. The case had to be shoehorned because of my difficult schedule, but the group was ready and they wanted direction now! I also brought along a friend of mine, Lucy. She was in her early fifties and I'd met her a couple of years before when she had gone through treatment for her own obesity; now she was recovering wonderfully. We all met at Jill's apartment and redefined what was presented on the conference call, then traveled as a caravan over to her parents' home.

The house was a typical ranch-style lazing in the desert air with a pool in the back and all the books and school stuff and piles of living that a house of five near-adult children manifests. It was cool inside and, at first, I felt refreshed. But then I realized the darkness of the interior accounted for the temperature more than the air conditioning. It was a darkness that was clearly more than a matter of covered windows and dim lighting.

There were fifteen of us (husband, six children, myself and my guest, parents, and a couple of close family friends) huddled around the living room when Doreen wheeled herself unsuspectingly into our presence. Realization was immediate and she never stopped turning the wheels of her chair—just changed direction and left the room. I was sure that if there had ever been a time when she had wished she had use of her legs, it was at that moment.

I sent Jill and her grandmother, Doreen's mother, into the other room after her. They had been appointed the "diffusers" during our preparation. It's always difficult to wait in such times and I was getting concerned because it seemed to be taking a long time to convince her just to come and listen. Just as I approached the door to the other room, I overheard Doreen saying, "I just don't care anymore."

Gently, I persuaded her to come back into the living room just to hear us out; we were only there because of how much they all loved her. We went around the room slowly but I could tell the group was losing heart as we went; Doreen's wall of apathy was standing too formidable against them. I decided she needed something only someone who had been where she was now to convince her that there could be a time when she would care again. I introduced Lucy and watched her kneel down in front of Doreen, putting her hands gently over Doreen's tight fists.

"I know how you feel. Look at me," she commanded softly. "I know how you feel; I lost 311 pounds over a five-year period. It's true and it's a possibility for you!"

Doreen's eyes blinked, sending two big tears down her full, round cheeks. "Let's go," she whispered.

"YES!" everyone shouted in unison, jumping out of their seats! You'd have thought we'd been watching the Super Bowl and our team won. It was a moment I'll never forget and an experience that reminded me how important it is sometimes to have someone in the intervention who can truly relate to the addicted person's plight. I'm sure I couldn't have achieved the same results without Lucy's being there; it made me grateful for others in the world who take it upon themselves to share their success with no thought of reward. It reminded me of why I'm in this business.

Doreen immediately went to a treatment center for eating disorders in Arizona. Our intervention was five years ago and I'm happy to report Doreen is very much an active part of her family's life; in fact, from what I've heard, some of the kids are having a hard time keeping up with her now!

I have often stated that without the solution, I could not intervene. Much thought and care goes into choosing the right treatment center for the patient and family. In other words, recommending the best course of treatment is essential.

THE COURSE OF TREATMENT

The treatment is a haven, a place for healing, where people who have difficulty overcoming denial of their addiction or passivity about confronting it can be guided in taking essential steps toward restoration of their physical, spiritual, and mental well-being. The following is a generalized description of the components of a good comprehensive treatment center program and a list of things families and others may want to discuss with intake counselors on the phone or during a personal tour of a facility.

Pre-admission: This includes verifying insurance coverage, determining payment obligation, completing release forms for medical information and for confidentiality, physical status, problem areas, etc.

Intake and Admissions: Even with thorough preadmission arrangements, there are often unexpected questions or insurance documents that need to be addressed. And because of their emotional and/or physical state, patients may be resistant to answering questions, so this interval can be critical in shaping patient attitudes. Most treatment centers do have empathetic staff members who make the admission process as painless as possible.

Primary Care/Detoxification: The medical aspects of addiction are focused on during primary care/detoxification, so the environment of the detoxification unit (where the patient is first assigned) is very clinical. Some facilities have a walking detox; as the patient is participating in the counseling, he is also being monitored for vital signs and medication needs, tests are interwoven, and orientation needs are addressed. The patient's primary counselor introduces himself to the patient on the first or second day and conducts psychological/sociological tests to establish treatment priorities. Specially skilled nurses or counselors are often assigned to spend private, one-on-one time talking to new patients in an effort to ease their fear and anxiety.

Some patients experience a surprising surge of physical well-being after withdrawal and think they're ready to leave—problem solved. The staff, as well as family members, must unite with the patient's case manager to motivate the patient to remain in treatment. When a patient leaves against medical advice, he is very likely to have another chemical dependency crisis within a short time, and then the patient might decide to get further help immediately after the crisis. But there is a major risk that he might not ever get help and eventually succumb to the disease.

Time spent in primary care or detox is usually two to four days, depending on the severity and physical effects of the addiction.

Rehabilitation: This is the heart of the inpatient program—time, space, and empathy to attain attitudes of admission and compliance that will ensure the patient's recovery. Jobs, financial obligations, relationships, holidays, and the rest of the world are not allowed to intrude. Patients are expected to follow a daily routine designed to foster self-discipline and help them accept responsibility for their own mental and physical well-being.

Some of the things included in the routine are: doing their own laundry, keeping their rooms neat and clean, taking part in recreational therapy, one-on-one counseling with the primary counselor, focusing on overcoming fear and frustration through self-exploration, doing written exercises, participating in group therapy sessions, attending educational classes, meditating, becoming aware of the spiritual concepts behind the 12-Step programs, attending same-sex therapy sessions, participating in family counseling, interacting with others, and becoming involved with an ongoing self-help community support group.

Aftercare: This stage begins when the patient leaves the treatment center and resumes his daily activities. Remember, treatment gives you a road map to recovery—but you must follow the map or you'll get lost! Many treatment centers offer aftercare sessions one night a week for as long as a year after inpatient treatment ends. These sessions not only reinforce the regimen and activities begun during rehabilitation, but also strengthen connection to an anonymous self-help group separate from the treatment center, a connection that is essential to many people to ensure their continued progress toward recovery. If you are from another state, the treatment center will explore aftercare in your state to make a comfortable transition.

Things to Consider about the Treatment Center

The Treatment Facility

You should definitely tour the facility. Is it cheerful and clean? Are the patient's living accommodations attractive? The ambiance, the grounds, and the view are meaningful only insofar as they may instill or increase the confidence and positive feelings of patients and/

or their families. (Many facilities have videos of their programs that they will send out to you immediately upon request.) Notice the geographical location—is it within easy reach of the family for family counseling? You might want to know if a psychiatrist is on staff; they are not on staff at all treatment centers. Ask if the patient can be evaluated, if necessary. When a psychiatrist is not on staff, the treatment center usually has someone who comes in on a contract basis. Find out what type of clothing patients should bring and when the visiting hours are. What are the hours of the admitting office?

THE STAFF

The general attitude of any staff member should point to his or her philosophy that encompasses the physical, psychological, and spiritual well-being of patients. A rule of thumb: If you do not receive immediate positive feedback from any staff member you encounter when visiting a facility, that person is not doing his job. It's unfortunate when a family member is made uneasy by a staff member who behaves unprofessionally or otherwise falls short of the visitor's expectations, but a single individual's shortcomings should not make you conclude the facility is not a good one. Speak to an administrator about any doubts or uneasiness you experience.

Other things you may want to know about the staff and the facility are: their average length of service at the facility, the percentage of patients who have completed treatment, the number of staff members recovering from addiction themselves, or who have been co-dependency enablers and/or are adult children of alcoholics, what the counselor/patient ratio is (1:6 or 1:8 is good, 1:10 is acceptable), and how calls from employers or business associates are handled by staff.

DETOXIFICATION

Some things you want to know about the facility regarding their detox procedures are: how long the doctors and nurses in the detox unit have been working in the field of chemical dependency, do they wean patients off detox medication as quickly as possible, does the detox staff encourage patients to be aware of the longer-term aspects of recovery while treating them medically, and whether the results of the patient's physical examination at the center are made available to the spouse or significant other.

REHABILITATION

Here you want to know what techniques the primary counselor uses to achieve bonding with the patient, what psychological or sociological tests are used, and whether mood-altering drugs are administered during rehab—they shouldn't be. Also, find out the frequency of one-on-one sessions with the primary counselor, what the daily schedule is during rehab, if a nutritionist is on staff, if there is vitamin therapy available, whether or not the dietary plan is available for review, what physical and recreational activities are available, the types of spiritual guidance offered, and how many days the average patient is in rehab before family counseling begins, and how often family sessions are held. Who will the family therapist be and what responsibilities will family members be expected to assume for themselves during counseling? You might also want to know if four-hour passes are given and how successful they have been.

AFTERCARE

Regarding the patient's care after treatment, these are some of the things you want to know about. Is there an aftercare program? If so, how often are meetings held and what are they focused on? Does the program include both patients and their families—separately, together, or both? Check the rate of attendance at aftercare programs. Is a connection to one of the anonymous self-help groups separate from the treatment center encouraged? Beyond aftercare, does the treatment center have an alumni group?

Alumni groups are very important in the continuance of full recovery and bonding with families who share their strength and hope. Please remember that there are different models of treatment today, especially designed due to budgetary factors, insurance companies, and (the new buzz word) "rapid stabilization," in and out. When choosing a treatment center, have a professional assist you for best overall packages that include the family, patient, physical and budgetary factors.

Treatment facilities work. I do believe that if time is taken out to address these areas (and choose the most appropriate place), the reward of the patient staying, completing, and attending aftercare is well worth the time and effort. For those out of state, the aftercare counselor will find the appropriate connections in one city, that is, alumni group, therapist, outpatient program.

VIGNETTE—.44 MAGNUM

"Just a minute," I heard Mary Margaret (my assistant in the outer office) say. I hadn't been aware of the soft hum of her voice while she spoke at length to the other person on the phone until it stopped. The silence shouted at me and I waited for her to come into my office. I knew she had been speaking to a potential client.

"She says they can't wait," Mary Margaret told me. "The situation is getting too dangerous. I think you'd better speak to her directly."

"What's the scenario?" I asked.

"Mrs. Todd is on the phone, calling about her fifty-one-year-old son, Joe, who's addicted to crystal meth. He's borrowed and stolen from friends and family and sold practically everything he owns, and he still owes a bundle to a couple of local dealers in Seattle. That's where Mrs. Todd is calling from. She's afraid he'll kill himself even if he manages to escape the clutches of the dealers who are after him."

I nodded. It was a story I had heard before, but no less traumatic for its familiarity. Mary Margaret closed the door on her way out as I lifted the receiver off the phone.

"Mrs. Todd," I said with a confidence I later lost somewhat during this case. "This is Ed Storti, how can I help you?"

I did my assessment over the phone as we talked for over the next two hours. It was a Thursday afternoon and we scheduled the preparation for Saturday morning and the intervention for that same afternoon. So much for the weekend of writing I'd planned; I'd have to do it while I was airborne up to Seattle.

Saturday was a typically gray morning in Seattle, cool and overcast—a nice change from the heat of Southern California for me, but I was far from cool and collected inside. Sometimes I think I get too optimistic and enthusiastic for my own good. The whole time Mrs. Todd was relaying information about her son fighting his way to oblivion with street thugs and criminals, besides his problem with narcotics, I was busy planning our gift to Joe as if it were a special anniversary. Because of my experience and the thousands of cases I've handled or participated in, I was sure this little demonstration of love would have Joe in a treatment center by the end of the day.

Borris, Joe's uncle and Mrs. Todd's brother, met me at the airport and drove us to his office near Pike's Place, the local fresh food marketplace. We met the others in his boardroom for the preparation and after they wrote the encouragement letters to be sent with him to treatment, we all went over to Mrs. Todd's house. It was a nice-sized, two-story wood house set well off the road in a small neighborhood fringing the east side of Seattle. Everyone sat down nervously, and I could tell they were reviewing everything I had crammed into their heads earlier.

Joe walked in and the nerves took on an electric pulse. He had a naturally bold presence, but being as hyper and agitated as he was that day, it was almost menacing. It was only his obvious confusion and fragmented thinking and speech that softened the threat of violence he was so near to all the time. He spoke with hands and great volume, and although he wasn't actually much taller than I, he seemed to loom over all of us. I remember making the sign of the cross over my heart beneath my coat before taking it off and getting things started. I braced myself for an uphill battle.

Joe listened to everyone speak—his two sons and two daughters, his wife, myself, and his mother and uncle—without interrupting. I was surprised at that. He couldn't keep still; he'd sit down and twist and turn, shift all around in his chair, get up and walk around, glance at us for mere seconds at a time, and then, suddenly, he said, "I'll go."

Normally, those are the words I'm always praying for, but here I could see that his willingness was not quite right and I started replaying in my head the things that had been said, and it dawned on me.

"Please allow me to explain treatment, Joe," I cautioned him. All the protection and love and warmth and care offered through a treatment center had translated into a getaway (from the streets, from his bill collectors, from the guys who wanted to bust his legs, from everything), which is why Joe had quickly accepted. "I don't want you to think the treatment center is easy, because they really ask you to open up and find yourself. There is some regimentation—get up in the morning and work out issues of addiction and a destructive lifestyle. The minimum stay at this treatment center is three to four weeks, Joe," I warned him.

Joe sat down and sat still for the first time. He leaned forward with his elbows on his knees and rested his head on the backs of his hands and stared at me, daring me to continue. I glanced briefly at the others and understood their anxiety. Here he was willing to accept the gift they offered, the gift I had instructed them in how to give, and here I was telling Joe every reason he should rethink his quick answer of yes to treatment.

They had trusted me, they followed all my instructions, they got what they came for, and now it seemed I was unraveling it all. But I had to make sure Joe understood what treatment would demand. I have some people say yes to treatment and then, when they get to the center, they think they're going to Club Med. Helping the patient be realistic about the treatment center is as much a part of my job as helping someone get to treatment.

All this time, Joe continued to stare; he didn't say anything. Then, suddenly, he rose and left the room. I thought he needed to regain his composure; he was gone for about one minute and returned with an old, green canvas bag, and pulled out a .44 Magnum. Everyone caught his breath at once in scared surprise. No one said anything. I remember one of the chairs squeaking as one of the family members rocked back and forth ever so slowly to maintain composure.

"I'm going to go to treatment," Joe said. "I know I can make it work for me." The words sounded good, but by now Joe had pulled the heavy pistol from the sack and was caressing its barrel, turning it from side to side in admiration. We didn't know what to expect. Joe took two slow steps over to his brother.

"Here," he said. "Keep this for me. This is Little Pepe; you take care of Pepe while I'm gone and don't sell it."

And with that, we all began breathing again. I heard the gardener next door using the leaf blower, saw the sun breaking through the clouds, and I knew Joe was serious about treatment. It was over. The intervention was over, the moment of terror was over, and, for the family, a big chapter of their suffering (and Joe's) was also over. As it turned out, Joe did stick with his treatment program and is leading a healthy, peaceful life of recovery today. I've heard he's a counselor in a new recovery home. *Miracles do happen!*

Summary

So there it is in a nutshell—the honorable approach to motivational intervention as I see it. My goal is to be an instrument used to motivate patients into a treatment program, to remind them of how much they are loved and missed (as a healthy part of the family) and to instill the hope they think is lost.

Not every case warrants an intervention, not every case would benefit; that's why the family and the intervention specialist must go through the preliminary steps. First, the inquiry: Do we need to intervene? Then the assessment, the specialist's review of the situation: the type of addiction, sensitive issues, health and mind set of the patient, the support of the family, the financial considerations, the urgency, the plan and risks, etc. If an intervention is deemed appropriate and beneficial, the preparation is next. Many things need to be covered: the purpose, goal and process of the presentation, the logistics, the specific things that will need to be said or presented to the patient, particulars, the treatment facility alternatives, etc. Finally, the actual intervention or gift to the patient is presented. It likens a surgical procedure and must be done with extremely gentle, caring precision to be effective. All the participants are assistants to the surgeon (the intervention specialist), who must coordinate the abilities and energy of everyone present to have the most beneficial effect on the patient.

Being allowed to complete the presentation is the true goal of the intervention; if the patient goes to treatment, that's wonderful, but there is first a matter of being able to address the patient. It's so important for the participants to be able to say aloud how much they love and respect the addicted person and have the opportunity to encourage him or her to get treatment. A tremendous amount of inner work, time, and coordination effort goes into planning an intervention—it is a testament of the participants' love for the person. They deserve to be heard out.

There is also a risk involved. The possible reaction of the patient is feared, often with good reason. And although there is no guarantee the intervention will lead to immediate treatment, it does nearly 95 percent of the time. The intervention is often the "last chance" hope for the family; they must do this to know they've "done all they can." Yet, if it works, if the patient goes to treatment, the intervention is only the beginning. There is no cure.

Once the secret (of the addiction and its effects on the family) is out, no one in the family can return to old habits with the same (un)consciousness they had before. The entire family is changed by the public announcement and every member of the family must commit to getting on with their own lives, regardless of what the patient does. In this respect, the intervention is for the family even more than for the patient.

It's important for the family to be aware of the risks but they must also consider the potential danger, by comparison, of allowing their lives to center around the addiction. Even when an intervention is done and fully successful, in that the patient goes to treatment, the whole family needs to be committed to aftercare for themselves and the patient. Aftercare may consist of personal therapy, anonymous groups, self-analysis, and learning with journals and books or tapes, etc. Old habits are hard to break, but they're much easier to modify when you understand how they evolved in the first place and can see how they're no longer desirable for you now.

Addressing the needs of the patient, I only touched upon some of the available treatment program and facility options in this book. The information should serve as a springboard for your own search for the plan best suited to your needs.

The main thing I wanted to convey in this book is that help (hope) is out there and you're not alone. I believe the "kinder, gentler" approach is the most effective route where interventions are concerned and that your sincerity in wanting to reclaim a chemically dependent loved one from the disease of addiction is truly an honorable gift—for them as well as for yourself. Be proud of yourself for loving enough and caring enough to try to help—that's the critical key for all of humanity. I applaud you for your courage and unconditional love!

God bless,
Ed Storti

SUBSTANCE ABUSE CENTERS

The following is a list of treatment centers and medical corporations that provide comprehensive care, have interventionist specialists on staff, or will make referrals to outside interventionists. This list is· not all-inclusive by any means; there are many additional treatment centers with qualified interventionist specialists on staff.

Betty Ford Center
Rancho Mirage, Calif.
1-800-854-9211
1-619-773-4100

Caron Foundation
Wernersville, Penn.
1-800-678-2332
1-215-678-2332

Cottonwood Centers, Inc.
Tucson, Ariz.
1-800-877-4520
1-602-743-0411

DePaul Hospital
Milwaukee, Wis.
1-414-281-4400

Father Martin Ashley
Havre de Grace, Md.
1-301-273-6600

Harmony Foundation Inc.
Estes Park, Colo.
1-303-586-4491

The Hazelden Foundation
Center City, Minn. & Fla.
1-800-257-7800
1-612-257-4010

Hollis Institute
Los Angeles, Calif.
1-800-8-ENOUGH
(eating disorders)

Hyland Center
St. Louis, Mo.
1-314-525-1200

Las Encinas Hospital
Pasadena, Calif.
1-818-795-9901

Mayo Medical Center
Rochester, Minn.
1-507-255-4122

The Meadows
Wickenberg, Ariz.
1-800-621-4062

The Menninger Foundation
Topeka, Kans.
1-913-273-7500

Merrit Peralta Institute
Oakland, Calif.
1-415-652-7000

New Beginnings
Lakewood, Calif.
1-800-451-1131

The Palm Beach Institute
West Palm Beach, Fla.
1-305-833-7553

Promises
Los Angeles, Calif.
1-310-390-2340

Provo Canyon School
Provo, Utah
1-800-848-9819

Spencer Recovery Center
Anaheim, Calif.
1-714-991-4673

Rancho L'Abri
San Diego, Calif.
1-619-463-0211

Springbrook
Newberg, Oreg.
1-800-333-3712

San Pedro Peninsula Hospital
San Pedro, Calif.
1-310-514-5300

St. Helena A.C.R.P.
Deerpark, Calif.
1-800-454-4673

Scripps Memorial
La Jolla, Calif.
1-619-458-4300

St. John's Hospital
Santa Monica, Calif.
1-310-829-8905

Serenity Lane
Eugene, Oreg.
1-503-687-1110

Talbott-Marsh Recovery Campus
Atlanta, Ga.
1-800-445-4232
1-404-994-0185

Sierra Tucson
Tucson, Ariz.
1-800-624-9001
1-602-624-4000

Willing Way Hospital
Statesboro, Ga.
1-912-764-6236

Smithers Alcoholism
   Treatment & Training Center
New York, N.Y.
1-212-523-6491